Morley Marvels

MORLEY MARVELS

RobertMorley

MEMOIRS, NOTES, AND ESSAYS OF THE
FAMED ACTOR, RACONTEUR, COLLECTOR,
HOTEL GUEST, AND MAN OF LEISURE

SOUTH BRUNSWICK AND NEW YORK
A. S. Barnes and Company

©1976 by Robert Morley

A.S. Barnes and Co., Inc.
Cranbury, New Jersey 08512

FIRST AMERICAN EDITION PUBLISHED 1979

Library of Congress Catalogue Card Number: 79-50770
ISBN 0-498-02397-4

PRINTED IN THE UNITED STATES OF AMERICA

Editor: Sheridan Morley

Contents

Such Stuff As Dreams Are Made On . . . .

Bêtes Noires

Far-Away Places With Strange-Sounding Names

Private View

Reflections in a Dressing-Room Mirror

Preface

Robert Morley is a gift to any editor with deadlines to worry about. He is ready to tackle any subject and always delivers on time. Humorous writing is rarely as easy as it looks but Robert always gives the impression that, for him, it requires no effort at all. His conversation, of course, is exactly the same: he has opinions on everything and expresses them with fluency and style. No wonder that he is as popular with talk-show hosts as he is with editors, filmgoers and theatre audiences.

In America, where he is much admired, Robert Morley is regarded as everything an Englishman should be – sophisticated, witty, a trifle eccentric, stylishly fond of tradition and the Good Things in life. Matrons swoon over his accent and jumboloads of American tourists arrive each summer to see Morleyland. Many are surprised and disappointed that we don't all look and talk like him. One can't really blame them. In an age of increasing conformity Robert remains defiantly larger than life, in every possible sense. He is both rebel and traditionalist: rebel in his contempt for Big Business and many Establishment attitudes, traditionalist in his love of the English countryside, the monarchy, club life, and the theatre. He is a great traveller, with an insatiable curiosity about the way other people live, but will tell you – at length – that any Englishman who chooses to live elsewhere is either a knave or a fool.

Many of the pieces in this, the second anthology of his writing, first appeared in *Punch* and I am truly delighted that he has been such a prolific contributor – as well as a most entertaining companion at the Punch Table. A few years ago he agreed to become our food critic and some of his best articles are included in this volume. Robert not only looks like a man who enjoys good food and wine (always an encouraging sign in a critic) but also writes about the subject knowledgeably and with the gusto he brings to everything he does.

One sometimes wonders what would have happened to him if he had gone into politics. He *looks* every inch a Minister; indeed he is far more convincing in the role than any of the people who are actually in the Cabinet. But I suspect he would have hated the straitjacket imposed by political convention. His highly-developed sense of the ridiculous would have been a formidable handicap rather than the asset it so obviously has proved to be in his chosen career. He would have remained a maverick, an outcast. But he would cut a splendid figure in the House of Lords and I, for one, would love to see him there one day.

It says much for Robert's skill that it is hard to be angry with him even when he seems to be talking nonsense. His political views (and particularly his admiration of the Soviet Union) strike many people as naive and his love of argument frequently leads him to make statements which he knows to be absurd but which invariably achieve their primary objective: to stimulate discussion. Impatient with small talk, he likes to provoke others with emphatic and sometimes outrageous pronouncements. But he is never dull or pretentious, and he disarms adversaries by making critical comments on his character before they have a chance of doing so. 'I am not a reasonable man,' he says. And 'I am not a good listener.' He even concedes that he sometimes makes a fool of himself. How *can* one be angry with a man like that?

WILLIAM DAVIS

**MORLEY
ON
MORLEY**

The Scuttlebut

At a party the other evening I was taken to task by my host. 'The story you have just told,' he chided, 'I found excruciatingly dull and almost certainly inaccurate. It's not as if you had attended the funeral, or even been asked to do so. You don't, I imagine, know Princess Margaret.'

'I don't have to know Princess Margaret,' I retorted, stung by his sudden venom, 'I was merely recounting a remark made to Her Highness. I am sorry, I thought it would amuse you.'

'It doesn't. I cannot abide gossip.'

To say that I was shocked by his attitude is an understatement. As far as I am concerned, to tell me he doesn't like gossip is like someone telling me he doesn't like Queen's Pudding. I simply cannot understand it, nor do I approve.

In my dictionary, gossip is defined as idle talk or rumour about the private affairs of others. It lists 'scuttlebut' as an alternative. I learnt to scuttlebut in early childhood, and have been at it ever since. One of my uncles wore stays. If you hugged him in a certain place, you could feel the whalebone. He must have thought me an affectionate child, but having spread the rumour, I was forever trying to verify the fact. At school, at least the ones I went to, there was a tremendous amount of scuttlebut about sex, some of it fairly inaccurate, but none the worse for that. In an effort to dispel surmise, the headmaster used to entertain chaps who were leaving for public schools to a final briefing. Not a good scuttlebut himself, he contented himself at the session I attended with chalking up on the blackboard the imperishable phrase, 'Smut is rot'. I never had any intention of heeding his parting admonition to refrain from discussing the matter further. I have always wanted to know who is going to bed with whom. I suppose I feel that in some ways it enables me to see more clearly the shifting patterns of life. It doesn't, but no matter.

I like, too, knowing how much money people left, what exactly they died of. I have a friend whose morbidity on this count exceeds my own almost to the point of madness. He spends most mornings with *The Times* obituary column in one hand and the telephone in the other, trying to contact distant relatives or casual acquaintances of the listed deceased, to verify what finally carried them away from us.

'Surely,' he will say, 'you knew Mrs. Perkins?'

'No,' I tell him.

'But I am almost certain I met her at dinner at your house once. Mrs. Perkins. She lived in Oswestry, you must remember her.'

'No,' I tell him, 'why?'

'She's dead. I have an idea she had a weight problem. It could have been heart, I suppose. What do you think?'

'I have no idea,' I tell him, but before the end of the morning he is usually back on the blower. 'It was angina,' he informs me reproachfully. He believes I don't take sufficient interest in other people, but of course I do. I am passionately interested in other people. I can't wait to find out what everyone is up to. If I think it's worth repeating and it's not actionable, be sure, gentle reader, that you will be the first to hear.

The Collector

From time to time I have wandered into Sotheby's, playing at being a connoisseur. I have purchased a catalogue at the door and stared at the paintings on the walls. I have never actually plucked up sufficient courage to ask to hold an object of vertu in my hand, but I have examined the folly of Fabergé at a respectful distance. In one of the many houses I shared with my parents years ago, we had a specimen table, a small oval affair on which the objects displayed were protected by a glass top. There were one or two miniatures, a silver coach, a Victorian châtelaine and a parasol handle by the master himself, but not much else. In Sotheby's I have a special expression I adopt when I think anyone is watching. Only I know whether this Vermeer is genuine and no one is going to call my hand, it says.

In the sale-room itself I am circumspect and motionless, always apprehensive lest by some involuntary movement I acquire a porcelain horse or a commode. I am happy in Sotheby's because there is little I want and seldom anything I could afford. Not having bought Lot 185 for seventy-five pounds I am, I argue, seventy-five pounds better off. It must be terrible to be a collector, to go round the world seeking pieces of milk glass and finding them, at a price. In point of fact I do collect silver donkeys, but find my enthusiasm impaired. I am beginning to think I shan't ever buy another. In my youth I once owned a stamp album, but I was and still am extremely clumsy and impatient with inanimate objects, and I soon tired of sticking in the stamps on the wrong pages and trying to detach them again without tearing them.

With an hour to kill in a strange town I, like everyone else, search out the antique shop, unless the pub is open. There must be something about living with sixteen cupboards at the same time that induces resignation. All antique dealers share this curious detachment, or is it I who have the same effect on each of them? They don't seem to expect me to buy anything. My arrival interrupts them apparently, but from what task?

15

They seem to have just stepped out of old-fashioned motor cars and not yet had time to undo the cords that bind the refectory table to the roof. Like racehorse trainers, they are always on the move.

In inspecting the stock, I ignore the goods on display; hidden in a dark corner, I tell myself, is the treasure I seek, but how will I recognise it? I know the dialogue once I have done so, of course.

'That old lamp, how much would you want for that?'

'I didn't even know I had it. Take it for fifty pence. It's no use to me.'

After that I only have to carry it ouside and rub. But to rub what? Ah, there's the rub. Would I recognise a Renoir or a sixteenth-century wassail cup? Unlikely; more than unlikely – unthinkable. Why then do I waste my time? Why do I pause, once over the threshold, and listen with such pleasure to the jangling of the bell and the footsteps of the approaching proprietor? Why do I long to be confronted with age in a cardigan? When I come face to face with anyone young and obviously on the ball, I cut short my visit. What I am really looking for is a victim. If there is to be a wide boy, it's got to be me.

Of course, it's different if you're selling something, as I was the other morning. I arrived early. Sotheby's had hired the gold chairs and the television set. The catalogues were over two pounds, but I had brought the one they had already posted to me. One of the perks is not having to pay for a catalogue. You also get a chair reserved, but I didn't sit on mine. I perched at the back on a table. I thought some dealer might be made a shade more comfortable, might even stay longer and bid for my lot, which came on at the end, more or less. My lot was a Utrillo. I had bought it casually one day out of a window in Bond Street when I had decided to turn myself into a company. In those days it was a fashionable tax ploy. It didn't work, of course; no tax ploy ever really works. If it did it would mean the end for chartered accountants. If there was a Golden Mean, a guaranteed panacea against tax, how simple life would be, and how happy. I bought the picture for my boardroom, not so well furnished as some, being just a shack in the garden. I didn't hang it there. I was always hoping to hold our annual general meetings in the drawing-room, where we could all admire my attempt to emulate Onassis. But the annual general meeting for some reason was invariably held at my accountants; and on the day when they wound up the company they asked about the picture, and it was suggested that I ought to sell it and give the proceeds to the Revenue. I didn't feel particularly aggrieved. I had looked at the picture for twenty years and was a bit sick of it.

In course of time, Sotheby's sent an expert to look at it himself. He didn't think it was the best Utrillo he had ever seen, but he did think it would fetch a good deal more than I had paid for it. I felt strangely proud. For once my art appreciation had been vindicated. Flushed with triumph I showed him another picture I had bought at about the same time, but lightning, it seemed, had as usual not struck twice.

On the appointed day I delivered the picture to Sotheby's and they took it into their custody with the casual sangfroid which distinguishes the firm. I left it propped against a door, along with its betters, waiting to have its photograph taken for the catalogue. The latter, when it arrived, was impressive. On the cover was a list of the vendors. I was delighted at my own billing. This is the sort of cast I have always dreamed of appearing with. The Viscount Astor, The Edward James Foundation, Mrs. Bernard Van Custem, Monsieur Clement Rouart of Paris, The Estate of the late Hugo Cassirer, and Me.

The best pictures of all, however, seldom disclosed the owner's name. The Provenance stopped just short of that. Who, for instance, was selling the Renoir? As it turned out, no one. It was bought in for just under three hundred thousand pounds, but most of the others sold, though not as well as had been expected. There were four Pissarros which went as one lot for two hundred and twenty thousand. The auctioneer gave no indication of whether the price was a triumph or a disaster. Neither, I suppose; just about average. How often, I wondered, did they sell four Pissarros on the same morning and all together, in one minute flat?

I suppose it's only money, after all. From the back it was difficult to tell where the bidding came from. Sometimes the buyer's name was announced, but as often as not, Mr. Wilson merely looked in someone's direction and nodded. Half way through the sale I dropped the top of my felt pen. For a good ten minutes I concentrated on recovering it. I was convinced it had rolled some distance and pursued it under everyone's feet. I didn't bob up too quickly, lest I should be mistaken for a bidder. While Manets and Degas were disposed of above my head, I crawled around unheeding. I needed the top, I told myself, needed it more than an Impressionist picture at that moment. Suddenly I found it on the pen itself. It hadn't rolled away after all. Something else must have dropped, but what it was I never found out. By the time my picture came under the hammer I was late for lunch. It fetched almost exactly what the expert had predicted.

I haven't the slightest idea who bought it. I don't miss it. I hope the Revenue will spend the money sensibly and are grateful that all those years ago I walked down Bond Street with an eye for a bargain.

The Hotel Guest

'I shall be needing a taxi in about ten minutes,' I told the splendidly-uniformed commissionaire in the hotel lobby at Fez.

'You are addressing,' he told me with extreme patience, 'the personal aide-de-camp to His Majesty, the King of Libya.'

We all make mistakes. I like it very much when I am taken for a salesman in Fortnum and Mason's. 'You must try these biscuits,' I tell the customer, opening the tin and popping one into his mouth.

In Split, once (how I get about), I couldn't locate the hall-porter – Yugoslavia was going through a phase of 'spot the workers'. When I eventually ran him down he was in shirt sleeves.

Normally, I am happy in hotel foyers; I like to sit with my foot pointed at some immovable object. Those who pass my imaginary photo-finish camera are counted meticulously. The twentieth, or possibly the nineteenth, is the one I am fated to change places with. 'Life,' I tell myself, 'will be happier if I step into the shoes of this young athletic tycoon striding towards a fortune.' Sometimes disaster strikes. I am not willing to change places with the shrivelled old lady – she may be richer than I, but money isn't everything. There are infinite variations: sometimes I don't change identities, just hats or teeth; sometimes I have to marry the girl or adopt the child. The most successful hotel lobby I ever came across was in Mexico City, where customers are seated as soon as they desire to register, and offered a glass of wine. It is at the outset that the harm is done or goodwill established. Life, for a hotel, begins just inside the revolving door – outside, sometimes, depending on how long the luggage takes on its mysterious, secret journey to the bedroom.

I fell in love with hotels just about the time I first read *Grand Hotel*. The Baron, the Ballet-Dancer, the Hall-Porter, the Jewel-Thief – are they still there? Is the Grand Hotel still there? Somewhere, surely, among the package-tourists, the conventioneers, the peripatetic sales-representatives, the lonely people still survive – the permanent incumbents holed up on their chosen floor, calling the waiters and the chamber-maids by their Christian names. Not all of them, of course; some hotels still boast their hermits – the guests whom no one sees, who clean their own rooms, take in their own trays, communicate with messages and bills pushed under doors. Not for them the games the rest of us play in the elevators. Here I am at a peculiar advantage as other visitors, sensing they have seen my face before, endeavour unsuccessfully to put a name to it. 'Haven't we met in Bath?' they ask. 'Or Lausanne? ... Aren't you in rubber?' 'Soap,' I tell them, 'and of course we know each other – I am often in Droitwich.' Leaving them puzzled, baffled, I step out before the penny can drop.

I am nervous of children in elevators – the ones who stand by the buttons, over-eager to press; the ones that giggle when the door opens in answer to their summons and have no intention of getting in. Come to think of it, I am nervous of lift-doors – how often, and quite unprovoked, have they tried to grab me; how often have I had to be rescued from their inexorable clutch by someone who understands the mechanism and can control the monster. I grew up with the sort of lifts which were worked by attendants pulling on a rope, or at least letting it run through their gloved fingers. Printed warnings as to the load gave a hint of the risk to be run. Each landing was an adventure – the slight adjustment to the floor level; the occasional refusal of the gate to open. There were the lifts, too, worked with a tram-handle mechanism, and the haunting terror of going right through the roof if the operator was to doze off and fail to release his grip. I am no more unsocial than the next fellow. It must be an awful life to travel perpetually between floors. Lift-operators have mostly passed into history, like pit-ponies, but I miss the gentle creatures.

It is true that foreigners get up earlier than we do. In the mornings, hotel elevators are full of spruce Swiss bankers and neat Norwegians, clutching slender briefcases and dressed meticulously with ne'er a handkerchief out of place, standing to attention as the lifts plunge downwards. They glance at their fellows and look away instantly, fearful of disturbing the train of thought which will carry them relentlessly through a day of significant and meaningful appointments. In the evenings, we may meet up with them again – their valises bulging with orders – travelling upwards towards their rooms and a solitary evening, confirming deliveries. The loneliness of the long-distance banker; a poignant reminder to the rest of us of the price of success!

Being an actor, I am also slightly irritated to leave a hotel at – or just before – curtain time and to observe the incredible number of people prepared to miss my performance on any one evening. Dressed in their glad rags, they appear oblivious of my appearance in their midst; hell-bent on enjoying themselves at some inane banquet or dance with fellow-members of their calling. Sometimes, when I return after my triumph to the otherwise deserted foyer, a small group of Master Bakers or Associated Footwear Traders are still standing each other double scotches, quite unrepentant of their folly, and even venturing to follow me into the elevator and along the corridor to continue the jollification in a suite adjoining my own. On such occasions, I am a stern upholder of the proprieties – the least squeak out of that lot and I am telephoning down to the night-porter with instructions to stop the rot.

I am not, I hope, on the whole, a spoil-sport where my fellow-guests are concerned, nor unmindful of the hospitality I have enjoyed over the years in hotels all over the world. I have been shushed by a barman in Kenya, anxious that I should not disturb antelope sampling the hotel salt-lick; and asked not to take photographs of students protesting in the Tokyo Hilton. I have been advised of curfews in Corunna by a hall-porter who expressed genuine astonishment when I heeded his warning and returned at the appointed time. I have leapt from my bath and run, dripping, into the garden during an earthquake in Istanbul, and found the chamber-maid calmly mopping the floor when I returned. I have left my passport with the desk-clerk in Salzburg and had it handed back to me, at the border where I crossed into Yugoslavia, the next day.

In a competition to find the perfect hotel guest, I suppose I wouldn't come high on the list. There are certain disciplines demanded these days which I prefer not to accept. I do not make out a breakfast-sheet and hang it on the door – I don't know how I am going to feel at breakfast-time. I don't vacate my room at noon but, if I remember, I do hang out a *Do Not Disturb* sign to prevent the chamber-maid pretending at seven o'clock she hadn't meant to wake me up so that she could start on the room as soon as possible. I try never to ask directions at the Desk – I find if I want to remember them I must stand outside, facing in the right direction at the start. Tipping is always a problem. I tend to give too much to the porter who initially installs me, not enough to the maid who looks after the room – but then she never seems to be around when I leave. I never quite manage the packing, or to leave enough time to lobby the accounts department. There are hotels nowadays which permit you to flourish your Credit Card at them and have the account forwarded. For some reason this particular concession is available at what they call 'the V.I.P. desk'. I suppose if there is one golden maxim for hoteliers, it is that there is no such creature as an N.V.I.P.

The Man of Leisure

All characters are imaginary, with the possible exception of my father, and bear no relation to any living member of my family or their friends.

We had a house once in the grounds of Wellington College, and my father decided to build a pool in the garden, in which he could keep goldfish, and even dug a few spadefuls before the jobbing gardener took over. When the time came to lay the concrete, we all weighed in. My father was not, strictly speaking, a do-it-yourself man. Something went wrong with the mix and the goldfish were always waking in the night, gasping for water. My father's design for the pool, like its construction, could be faulted, its proportions resembling a washbasin which had become detached from its pedestal. A year after it was completed, my father's marriage broke up along with his folly. No great harm was done by either event and it was simple to lift the pieces of concrete off the damp, beaten-down earth and hope the slugs would find a new home.

It was some forty years later that I was in a position to build a pool of my own, an altogether larger affair in which we could all swim. Up to that time I had taken my young to swim at my neighbour's. Rumour had it that he didn't like children, but I ignored the *canard*. He was a generous fellow, a man of the utmost good humour, and married into the bargain. If there was a cloven hoof concealed by the white flannels he habitually sported, I failed to observe it, indeed would have taken pains not to do so. It was inconceivable to me that he didn't look forward to our arrival to splash happily about in his elegant pseudo-Grecian folly. It is true he only heated the water at weekends and missed the brouhaha during the week when he was working away in town to earn the bread to buy the coke, for his was an old-fashioned boiler designed some years before the war, but Friday to Sunday we were in clover at a temperature of eighty and better.

As I say, I simply didn't believe he didn't like children, although sometimes I would admonish my chicks not to be quite so scream-happy. 'Mr. Neighbour,' I would tell them, 'doesn't really like . . .' – I couldn't bring myself to betray him completely – '. . . doesn't like children screaming,' I would finish lamely, as I threw their water wings onto the back seat and slammed the door.

It is the noise of the door slamming that I have come to dread in my turn, now I am older and wiser, disturbing the afternoon siesta beside my own water-hole. It could be the butcher's car in the drive or the postman's (mysteriously, we still rate two deliveries a day), or it could be my wife back from shopping, only I know she hasn't gone shopping. I close my eyes for the last ten seconds of bliss and open them, aware of the advance of the Pool Men. They come armed with flippers and rings and inflatable rubber monsters. Some of them even bring aqualungs and snorkel tubes. Some of them are already in swimming costumes, others disappear briefly into the house in search of a changing-room and a loo. The mothers, the au pairs, the house guests bring up the rear carrying baskets of food and clothes. Even if one doesn't have to rise to greet the children, it's a brave man who doesn't bestir when the grown ups start introducing each other.

'We've come to swim. I do hope you don't mind. This is Mrs. Armitage who's staying with us, and you know Bertha from Stockholm. George, say good afternoon to Mr. Morley, and Prudence, and this is their friend, Simon, and his friend Tiger, at least we call him Tiger.'

The children approach warily, anxious to have done with formality. They hurry away to dip their hands in the water and look reproachfully at me.

'It's colder than yesterday. Much colder.'

'It's been raining,' I tell them apologetically. Why the hell do I have to apologise for the rainfall?

The largest child always jumps in beside me.

'Not to splash,' comes a split second after the soaking.

'I am not sure whether Tiger swims or not,' says one of the mums cheerfully, 'but no doubt we shall find out.'

The mums don't swim, at least not right away. They like to talk and cover themselves with oil. One or two of them bring pencils and *The Times* crossword. The children demand an audience. 'Watch me, Mummy, watch me,' they shout and Mummy not only watches, but shouts back. She knows Sylvia can't hear under her bathing cap, so she shouts first to indicate that she wishes to communicate, and the second time, when Sylvia has temporarily disengaged her cap from her ear, because everyone else is shouting too.

22

I am a man who scoffs at those who wash their cars on Sundays in their drives, yet am a compulsive pool-cleaner myself. I really worry about the band-aids and elastoplast e'en now sinking to the bottom. I don't even like the way the children suck up the water and then expel it. When one of them complains that his eyes are stinging, I make a mental note to increase the algymycin as soon as the opportunity presents itself. After a few minutes the withdrawal symptoms start. Some of the young begin to shiver violently, some of the mothers to try and get their loved ones out of the water and into a towel. The exchanges begin with cajolery and finish in violent confrontation.

'Mummy says out, Roger. Daphne dear, I think you have been in long enough.' No child ever agrees. It is a point of honour to demand another few minutes, a last float to see who is shivering most. 'If you don't come out now I shan't bring you again.' Oh, if only I could believe it, if only Henry believed it, if only Mother herself believed it. 'If you don't come out now there'll be no television for a *week*.' The threats are empty. They always were, even in my own childhood. When the bathing finally stops, the children begin to think of things for me to do. 'Uncle Robert, will you get the croquet mallets? Mr. Morley, will you put up the swing? Can we see the skull which laughs? Where's the cat?'

'You are not to bother Mr. Morley,' the mothers insist. 'It's time for tea. I wonder if you have such a thing as a knife. We don't seem to have remembered to bring one for the cake.'

On my way back from the kitchen I observe the little groups picnicking on the grass. I am filled with remorse at my own inhospitality. 'There's food in the house,' I tell them, 'and chocolate biscuits and Coca Cola, and I can boil a kettle. It's no trouble.' Before I know what I'm saying we are all in the front garden. Only then do I discover I have already eaten the last Bath Oliver and we're out of bread.

When it's time to go home, everyone comes and thanks me and I beg them to come again whenever they would like to. I even urge the parents to make a plan for tomorrow, insist next time they bring even more of their friends and neighbours. Why, why? Of course the real reason I no longer swim myself is that I, too, am growing a cloven hoof.

HIGH
SOCIETY

By Appointment

Her Majesty Queen Elizabeth II, Defender of the Faith and a good deal more besides, is arguably the most expert monarch who has ever sat on the throne of Britain. I am not one of those who think that a throne is an uncomfortable seat, or that the life of a Queen isn't on the whole more rewarding and enjoyable than most. It must be bliss never to have to carry money and yet to be able to afford almost anything.

I have met her, I suppose, on half a dozen occasions in real life, and more often in my dreams. In the latter I am invariably the host and she appears to be in need of – or at any rate to welcome – advice. I awake with the pleasant but ephemeral sensation that I have put matters to rights once again in her country and mine. To listen to her on a more formal occasion, opening a school, or, less frequently these days, alas, launching a liner, one is conscious that she is not the girl to fling her bonnet over the windmill, she subdues the high spirits and the ready laugh, her smile is watchful, her demeanour purposeful, she is there to do the job she has been asked to do and she does no more and no less than the 'happening' warrants.

On less formal occasions she is altogether more approachable and a great deal jollier. She has a curiously reassuring and hearty laugh; she speaks her mind, I suppose, without the fear of contradiction. It may not be a remarkable mind, but there is no gainsaying that it belongs to a most remarkable and dedicated woman with whom it is a pleasure to take tea once a year at one of her Royal Garden Parties. I am not, of course, Her Majesty's sole guest on such occasions. She asks upwards of five thousand others, and most of them come. The invitations arrive in plenty of time to get propped up on the mantelpiece. Friends then know that we are busy on that particular afternoon and don't waste time asking us to tea with them. I am curiously forgetful about removing the elegantly-engraved card once the function is over. It is often still in place when it's time to put up the Christmas cards. With it come small admission tickets, a sticker for the car and directions for parking. The sticker has an X on it so that on the day you can leave the car almost anywhere. We chose the Mall this year, driving boldly up onto the footpath; another surge and we would have been in Green Park.

I am a lifelong opponent of the morning coat and grey topper, and although others sport them on these occasions, I and most of the Mayors wear civilian dress – in my case without a chain of office. Mayors and their wives go to Buckingham Palace Garden Parties in droves; so do Red Cross Officials, Embassy Staffs, County Councillors, Welfare Workers, Probation Officers and actors; anyone, in fact, who has led a decent, industrious and sober life working in and for the community and hasn't got a great deal to show for it except the engraved invitation, the car park badge and the tickets which have to be surrendered at the gate. There is a choice of gates but most prefer The Grand Entrance, which takes you into the Palace itself and out again pretty quickly, with just time to glimpse the china in the glass case, the portraits of some long-forgotten relatives, and the damask on the sofas. Bold spirits even sit down momentarily on the latter pretending to tie a shoe lace, but very soon Palace Life is over for the year (unless you decide to return the same way) and you are out through the French windows, to be confronted with the tents, the bandstands and the Gentlemen Ushers.

Impeccable is the word for the latter, though the tents in blue and white look pretty enough. The Gentlemen Ushers are distinguished by their umbrellas, which become ceremonial wands for the afternoon. It is their task to prevent a crush around the members of the family who are now about to essay singly, or in pairs, the two hundred yards' stroll across the turf which separates the terrace from the Royal tea tent, the enclosure within the enclosure, where they, too, will partake presently of tea, iced coffee, miniature éclairs, chocolate cake, and bridge rolls.

This is the walkabout originally introduced by Alfred the Great, and ever since refined and perfected by generations of Palace Guards trained to a ferrule. Their task at three–thirty when the gates open and the guests arrive, is to find in the throng exactly the right people, and more important, exactly the right amount of the right people to ensure a smooth passage of their charges across the sward. Too many, and the princess is impeded, too few and they face the chop. The ideal is a few steps forward, a pause while a bishop is greeted and polite chit-chat exchanged, a gracious dismissal of the gratified cleric and on to greet a privileged couple from the Guildford or Reading Chamber of Commerce. Royalty has to think fast, but the Ushers even faster. Inside their hats are the lists of those they hope to find in the crush. Each one must be approached discretely tapped on the shoulder (not, alas, with a sword, but with the brolly), and invited to stand still or move a little to the right and await the presentation. Gratified but self-conscious, the sheep await further instructions from the sheep dog. Others may move where they wish, secure an early cup of iced coffee, go listen to the band, even take a sortie around the lake and peer into the summerhouse, where the slide and the other toys are put away, but the chosen stand rooted in pleasure and anticipation, and presently the Royal Family comes out onto the terrace, the bands play 'God Save the Queen', and the various members are off, spreading themselves for our delight.

The Monarch has the lion's share of the crowd, naturally, and those waiting to be presented to her need considerable stamina and determination not to be nudged off course. They themselves have temporarily become part of the charmed circle – they stand their ground, smiling compulsively no matter how often their toes are stepped on. The tone is set by the officials who bend over backwards to ask the smallest favour. 'I wonder if you could possibly move back just six inches, or possibly nine, it would be most awfully kind? Thank you so much, that's perfect.' Elsewhere the crowds, standing on tiptoe – and one year, regrettably, even on chairs – to catch a glimpse of those they normally only meet on the television, are not quite so large. There is a little more time for the chat show, sometimes even too much, but Royalty is never at a loss and flatters outrageously.

'How nice of you to come, how lucky I am to meet you in this crowd. I envy you so much living at Burnham—on—Crouch. How sensible of you to choose to retire there.'

Circumstances and weather permitting, we stand, hat in hand, smiling inanely in the direction in which we think Her Majesty is probably moving, before going off to get our share of the cake. It may be only a small slice, and some of us have done a good deal more than the others to deserve it, but we all enjoy it. Afterwards, when it is over and the Queen has walked, briskly this time, back to the Palace, I like to linger beside those who are waiting for cars to pick them up. The loud speaker booms out all the way to Admiralty Arch . . . The Lord Mayor of Liverpool and Mrs. Brady, His Excellency the Dutch Ambassador, American Embassy Car Number Twenty, The Dowager Duchess of Builth, Mr. Bagbody. It is always Mr. Bagbody who intrigues. Why is he asked, who can he be? One of Her Majesty's Inspectors of Taxes, The Head of the Secret Service, a tramway employee from Blackpool completing a stint of twenty-five years' driving past the illuminations, a bird watcher from the Fens, a bank manager who has spent his leisure moments auditing the funds of a Society which protects windmills? Mr. Bagbody could be anyone as he stands there in his top hat and tails or his neat blue suit, his proud lady on his arm. It is 6.30 p.m. but in a moment he will be driven out of the Palace Gates; for him and for us, midnight is already striking.

Lunch at the Embassy

I paused on the doorstep of the great house in Belgrave Square, trying to remember the phrase which eluded me. As soon as I had rung the bell, and before the door opened, it came back to me. Political asylum, that was it. Should I tell them I had come to claim sanctuary? The trouble with actors is that they will dramatise. One step the other side of the Iron Curtain, and heaven knows what vistas open up. I had been asked merely to luncheon, but who could tell where it would all lead? Once inside the Embassy I was on foreign soil. Even the chance of kidnap didn't seem entirely remote. What if I chanced on some secret document, broke a code, discovered a high-powered radio transmitter when searching for the cloakroom? I must be careful, I told myself, if I'm to get out again.

The fellow in the white coat took my hat with just perceptible reluctance. If I was not expected, I had only myself to blame, having originally refused the invitation to meet a visiting Balkan playwright on his home ground. For one thing, I didn't speak their language, for another I had not heard of him, and in any case I make a point of refusing invitations relayed via my agents, unless of course there is a chance of money changing hands. I am not one for the cultural get-together. It is true we actors speak the same language, but it happens to be English. When asked to meet our colleagues from abroad, the proceedings are apt to be deadly. I don't know what happens at village dances these days – a good deal, I imagine – but when I was young, the boys stayed with the boys, the girls with the girls. At parties given by the British Council and similar functions, the English actors peel off at one end of the room and discuss their grosses, while the visitors search around for someone with at least a smattering of French.

Aware of the probable nature of the function, I had nevertheless changed my mind about coming because of the invitation card which arrived in my dressing-room by hand. On it someone had crossed out R.S.V.P. and written Aide Memoire. I found this phrase quite irresistible. If ever I was to speak the language of protocol, I decided now was the time. Besides, there must be some special reason for ignoring my earlier non-acceptance. I sensed this summons was at ambassadorial, I almost wrote conspiratorial, level. 'You're fishing in muddy waters, Morley,' I told myself, and putting on my Richard Hannay hat – it was Richard, wasn't it? – set off, and indeed arrived, albeit a little late.

I was the last one to be ushered into the vast drawing-room, and finding to my delight I was the only actor, proceeded as usual to put everyone at their ease. Their team included the Ambassador himself, a large, reassuring fellow with an almost uncanny resemblance to Leo McKern who usually plays the part on my television screen; his cultural attaché, who hastily withdrew to add, I suspect, another place card on the dining table; the playwright, and his friend. I never discovered what his friend did, and cast him instantly in the role of shadow. Our team was already cast – the Man from the B.B.C., the Man from the British Council, the Man from the Foreign Office, and the Lady from the British Museum, who was planning an exhibition for the spring. The Ambassador apologised courteously for the trouble he was giving the Museum authorities over security.

'No trouble,' the lady assured him, 'or rather, trouble we are happy to undertake.'

'I wouldn't send any of the stuff here if it's valuable,' I told His Excellency. 'Look what happens at Claridges.' I don't know why a draught of campari–soda invariably turns me into an *enfant terrible*.

Luncheon was made for me by a Charlotte Russe, a pudding of which I am particularly fond, and some delicious Balkan claret. I sat next to the playwright, who had started life as a head shrinker, but had taken up playwriting, and was, I gathered, more or less permanently employed by his local State Theatre to write light comedy. Like all good Communists, he wanted to know how much I got paid, and what was likely to happen to me when I got too old to act.

'I shall drop dead,' I told him, 'but in great luxury. We have, you know, a Health Service which is the envy of the world.'

'In our country, too,' he maintained stoutly.

By some extraordinary oversight, the British Council had failed to include my play on his cultural junket. I murmured condolences, and the talk turned on the difficulty of finding suitable play translators who do not insist on extra payment for adapting the piece. He threatened to send me some of his plays which had not been performed over here, and I retaliated. I gathered there were forty-two live theatres in his country, which is a small one, and a further twenty-eight in the Capital. Currently, Bernard Shaw's *The Millionairess* was drawing the crowds. *Waiting For*

Godot was also extremely popular, and all Anouilh's plays pack them in.

'Do you have television?' I asked, and trying to retrieve the brick before it fell on my toe, added pathetically, 'I mean, commercial television.'

'No, but we buy that from England,' I was assured. ' "The Forsyte Saga", and of course "The Saint". We buy from the Americans too, sometimes.'

Over the cigars and brandy I asked the Ambassador his opinion of the whole boiling. It wasn't a phrase with which he was familiar, but he rallied politely and for ten minutes did his best to acquaint a rather obstreperous and slightly over-elated British actor with the facts of international life as seen from his corner. On the whole it was the most lucid and optimistic appraisal of the world's predicament I have heard for a long time. He didn't envisage any more war or revolution than we were experiencing at the moment. Indeed, he thought it conceivable that the level of violence had already started to go down. He thought if we British were to accept our place in the world, and particularly in the Commonwealth, we could do a bit better than we were doing at the moment.

'What is our place?' I asked.

He shrugged his shoulders. 'The spirit of a country,' he told me, 'is sometimes more important than its size.'

I asked him about British politicians. 'You still have the cleverest business brains in the world. Believe me, I know. I am an economist before I am Ambassador.' It was the first time His Excellency's English had faltered, or had it?

I retrieved my hat, and stepped out into the sunshine of Belgrave Square. I must try and organise a Balkan holiday for myself, on the British Council if possible. I could do with some more of that claret.

À
LA
CARTE

Sloshing and Noshing

Bon viveurs have long bemoaned the fact that Lincolnshire by no means abounds in restaurants where haute cuisine has any real meaning. All the more praise, therefore, to Mr. and Mrs. Clew, who have just opened Harry's Place on the left bank of the Humber as you are fortunate enough to leave Grimsby on the way to Cleethorpes. On the day we called, the paint was still wet and Harry and his wife were enthusiastically redecorating. Selecting a table as far from the wall as possible, we decided on the £1.20 special nosh and were not disappointed with the hors d'oeuvre, although one sardine between two was perhaps a shade on the frugal side. However, the potato salad – with a heavy mayonnaise sauce in which I detected a hint of vinegar – was beyond criticism, and the apple peelings soaked in Mrs. Clew's own secret formula were a surprise. The salami was fresh cut and anchovies ringing a piece of cheddar cheese completed the dish. My wife chose widgeon à la Clew for her second dish, while I decided on a steak au poivre. We were in for our second surprise on discovering that the vin ordinaire was nothing of the kind. Apparently the entire family are keen – if amateur – vinophiles, and the carafe placed on our table was not only, we were assured, home bottled, but also home brewed. Instead of the more customary grape, which for some reason does not ripen satisfactorily in this part of the land, the Clews have experimented with varying success with other fruit extracts and the addition of surgical spirit, purchased in bulk. For dessert we tried the Pudding Ethel, named in honour of Mrs. Clew's mother. It turned out to be a cold saucer pancake with a raspberry blancmange filling. I haven't really felt at all well since.

Readers of the above will search in vain for Harry's Place, but they will, I hope, realise in time that I have joined the Clement/Egon/Ashley league as a slosh-and-nosh guide. I have been going round lately soliciting advice on where I should start. Nearly everyone has suggested Marks and Spencers. People are always telling me about Marks and Spencers. I don't mind so much in Britain, but when I go abroad it takes the gilt off the gingerbread of travel. In Toronto apparently no one shops anywhere else, or for that matter Hong Kong. Why then bother, I ask myself, to travel?

I walked all the way along Oxford Street, holding my umbrella aloft in a strong wind. Nothing slows me down more than the fear that my umbrella is going to blow inside out. The journey took forever. I found the food hall of Marks and Spencers in the basement; even the grapes were covered with cellophane, there seemed no way to taste anything. Various friends had cautioned me not to miss specific items. The chickens apparently are all free range birds, but naturally, ready for table, they don't look it. Shoppers darted around, selecting individual cottage pies. I thought how lonely everyone looked. Why, I wonder, does value for money always produce such a low pulse rate, except at the sales? I sighed for the Myer Food Halls in Melbourne, where the assistants' costumes are designed to complement the displays. Swiss Girls sell chocolate, Dutch Girls sell cheese, French Girls sell pâtisserie. I suppose there's no room or time for that sort of thing in our supermarkets. Selfridge's Food Department, across the road, was a great deal gayer. There was a queue at the bread counter, and no wonder. How important bread is to a nation, and how utterly are we betrayed in this country. If Mother's proud, she must surely be the only one. Last week I myself had tea out of a saucerless plastic cup off a plastic tray, and ate what tasted like a plastic Chelsea bun, at a service station off the M4. Everything, including the customer, was judged to be disposable. The national image is degraded by such places. I never thought I should be sorry for juggernaut drivers over from the Continent, but I am. I hope they bring sandwiches.

What Makes a Feast?

In a few months Britain will be dead. This will be the slump to end slumps – and the country. Eagerly predicted by practically all in the know and welcomed by some as a means of bringing the rest of us to our senses and them back to power. 'After the deluge – us!' is the heartening call of Mrs Thatcher and her merry band.

The fact that the theatres, shops and restaurants have seldom had it so good is merely a symptom of the disease about to decimate the rentiers, bankrupt Marks and Spencers, impoverish Harry Hyams himself. This is not the burgeoning of Spring, the colour brought back to the cheek of the invalid by returning vigour. It is the fatal flush before Death tears up the Social Contract; the final glass of champagne which cannot harm the patient, since he is practically dead already. 'Tighten your belts,' urge the politicians. 'Face up to reality,' screams Levin. 'How can we continue to spend what we haven't got?' I am reminded of those tireless sandwich-men who gather relentlessly where the action is – at Epsom on Derby Day, Hampstead Heath on Bank Holidays, and Piccadilly Circus when there is no great sporting event save dodging the traffic – and exhort us to 'Prepare to Meet God'. We may all have some explaining to do on Judgment Day but as we push and shove to get the money on, we pay scant attention to the Jeremiahs. If the penny drops, it drops into the slot-machine. When we're ruined we may kick ourselves that we squandered our patrimony, or just possibly that we have not. The soothsayers are having a field-day, but then, so are we. Whoever first said, 'Eat, Drink and be Merry', presumably spoke with his mouth full.

What makes a feast? Not, presumably, having to walk five miles there and back for a soup-plate of gruel. Yet there is merit, surely, in recalling the horn of plenty, the days of the Remove and the sorbet; the years of the locusts and the side dishes. It is no good pretending food hasn't helped me over the bad patches of life – I have as often been solaced by a bird on the table as one in the bed. Between gluttony and lust there has always been

39

unfair discrimination; to be a great lover is held altogether more estimable than to be a great eater.

At about the same time as I learnt there was no actual circus in Piccadilly, I learnt, too, that on the feast of St. Augustus the food at school was likely to be much the same as usual. Most parents are disposed towards boarding their young at establishments with a 'St.' in front as well as after the address on the envelope. It encourages them to think that the profits of the business may just conceivably be dedicated to improving the plumbing and not the headmaster's holiday home in St. (here we go again) Tropez.

I was unlucky to celebrate my feast-day in term time, which meant, unless I was fortunate enough to be paying one of my frequent visits to the San., sharing a small plate of chocolate biscuits and the cake sent by my mother with my friends. In point of fact, I never made any friends at school, even on my birthday. My neighbours ate the cake but seldom returned the compliment by offering a slice on their own natal days. I have ever since made a fuss of my birthday, puffing out the candles and enjoying the chocolate fingers with the children and grandchildren who, unlike my earlier playmates, ask me back in their turn.

The ritual feast has moved from the rain-forests of Fiji where, a few years ago, rumour had it there were still a few cannibals to be found enjoying their traditional fare. Rumour, as usual, was probably pulling my leg, but I did notice that Fijians do seem to enjoy at least looking at outstandingly fat tourists such as I, and estimating, possibly, how long I would have lasted in their great-great-grandfather's deep-freeze. But the great conglomerates check their spears in the cloakroom now, hang up their shields in the Connaught Rooms or the ballrooms of the hotels which cater to the Convention trade, assembling their tribe for a pow-wow before serving the *sole bonne femme*, the saddle of lamb, the pudding decked with icing-sugar, and the chairman himself proposing the loyal toast: 'You may smoke.'

How the chef must long, on the occasion of the Lord Mayor's Banquet, when he has refined the turtles and decapitated the boar, to place the glazed orange in the mouth of the Prime Minister or the Lord Mayor himself, and stop the rot.

Scraping the plate of memory to recall some of the memorable feasts I have attended I recall, alas, not the menus but the trivia: the opening bonanza at the Hilton in Park Lane – in the presence of Conrad Hilton himself – when the waiter, eyeing Mr. Getty at an adjacent table, advised our party to keep their handbags on the table and in vision; the three days'

40

feasting for the film-camera on a South Sea Island, with the stench of sucking-pig and rotten mangoes defeating the elegance of even Jean-Paul Belmondo.

There is a castle in Kent where you can buy yourself a feast, and you will be served by wenches dressed in Elizabethan costumes; and to taste royal venison and palfreys you will be drowned in Malmesbury wine; but you will be invited to sip it while watching a great hawk circle overhead high up in the rafters and swoop and carry upwards – regrettably, on the occasion I was present – not the proffered meat but a gentleman's personal rug, or, if you prefer such archaic terms, toupee.

But a feast is hardly a feast if you have to pay for it yourself. Let us return to the gritty-nitty of the title. A feast can be whatever you make it, wherever you enjoy yourself: lugging hampers stuffed with goodies to join the guns, or pocketing a few Marmite sandwiches for yourself and friend to be eaten on Paddington station in the intervals of writing down engine numbers. A feast can be the first fling when you stop going Dutch at the café and manfully pick up her bill as well as your own; or the last, with the table loaded with the funeral baked meats, and your friends telling each other how much you would have enjoyed the whole thing if only you'd been there. But, of course, you are.

I have left instructions for caviare and champagne. If there is one thing I – and, I sense, the country – is determined to avoid at all cost, it is the final extravagance of death duties.

The One-Up, Round-the-World Gourmet

He sat beside me at the bar and, when I enquired idly about his plans, he announced he was off to Strasbourg to eat a goose. So many travellers attempt too much. His reply encapsulated a singleness of purpose altogether admirable. I don't now remember to whom I was talking, only that it was in Buck's where such affirmations are – or at least were – listened to without distress.

How far is one prepared to go for a good meal?

I posed the question to several acquaintances. A number demanded elaboration: 'Do you mean a free good meal? How good is good?' Myself, I would be prepared to go a long way, but then, of course, I like travelling, let alone food. Clutching my Michelin, how often have I sought out the rosette and crossed spoons and demanded the speciality of the house and, strangely enough, how often have I been disappointed.

There is a Café de Paris in Biarritz which serves, for a few golden weeks of the year, a sort of special white truffle with apples, which I found as nasty as tripe and couldn't finish. The baby lamb at Les Beaux is, to my mind, altogether too babyish – a veritable slaughter of the innocents. Reminding me of a celebrated restaurateur in Gerard Street – now, alas, retired – who would explain the ritual murder necessary to prepare the feast he had in store for me. 'Mr. Morley, you take a baby frog just as he utters his first bellow, and cut off his head. You must do it in the moonlight, otherwise it is no use, and then you throw away everything but the tip of the heart where the coralete is' – there was always, in the description, a word I could not catch – 'then, later, you bake this for a dozen hours on a slow peat fire, turning it over and over, and then you butter it at the table.'

'If you want a really first-class moussaka,' I heard myself announce the other day, 'you'll have to go to Newbury.' The fellow who was unlucky enough to be within earshot hadn't even mentioned moussaka and, as far as I know, never touched the stuff.

We each have a Gourmet Guide hidden on our person and long to expose it. 'Don't be put off by the Formica tabletops,' we urge each other, 'the chef used to cook for Onassis before he took to the bottle.' We are speaking of the former chef, naturally – for we all know, Aristotle was teetotal.

The impression we seek to leave is of a blue tit which has already skimmed the cream. When the milk-bottle is taken inside it will not be the same. The eateries we extol today will, tomorrow, be ruined by the hoi-polloi – places we would not be seen dead in. 'Not quite what it was, is it?' we enquire of the still-faithful customer. 'I hear the *ptarmigan à la façon de Président Giscard* is pre-cooked and frozen.' Once the hat-check girl and the diners' club take over we are off, once more, in search of the little restaurant in Shrewsbury where the firemen eat because the captain's wife comes from Bayonne and does a mincemeat tart which is out of this world.

I have two distinct approaches when eating out. Quiet confidence, as host – a hint of formality in my manner of greeting the staff. I try to impart a sense of occasion to the ritual of seating my guest and choosing the food and wine, adding a touch of originality by asking for the salt to be taken away until we have need of it. 'I don't know if you feel as I do,' I remark to my friend, 'but I cannot bear a cruet with the aperitif.' The use of the word *cruet* here is, I flatter myself, not without courage. Occasionally, before ordering the meal I will summon a waiter and enquire about his wife. 'Better, I hope?' I tell him. I don't actually know whether the fellow has a wife but he will not care to correct me, though he may look a little puzzled – but I am confident that my companion will mistake his bewilderment for gratitude. The impression I wish to give – and, I have no doubt, succeed in giving, is that of the late Noël Coward in charge of a happy ship: the crew's troubles are my troubles – up to a point, of course. Before choosing the wine, I always say quite simply and, indeed, truthfully, that I know nothing whatever about it. When the others have suitably expressed their disbelief, I suggest we take the wine-waiter's advice. 'Something you want to get rid of,' I tell him encouragingly. 'Perhaps a Sancerre 1958, or Sauvigny de Clos Montard '49?' I usually give a little chuckle as he departs. When he returns with the bottle I am careful not to taste it – this is a privilege I reserve for my guest.

When our roles are reversed, of course I am a totally different creature. I go for the overkill. 'What a delightful bistro!' I exclaim. 'Blue beams! I don't think I've ever seen blue beams before *and* brown paper napkins! So convenient for the Natural History Museum – it's just round the corner, surely? How did you find it? Let's stick to the set meal, shall we? It's sure to be excellent . . . I'll have what you're drinking – half a carafe will be ample. How long has this place been going? . . . And I've never heard of it. What do you suppose they're having at the next table? Who would you say the people who come here are, mostly? . . . Students? It's so jolly and unpretentious. I am reminded of a little place half-way up the Bosporus on the right-hand side – you know it, of course – I was taken there by our Ambassador to eat yoghourt, and then we discovered this perfectly marvellous way they cook kid – in a blanket. You must try it next time you're there; just mention my name – or even the Ambassador's.'

Stored among the disorder of my memory is a positive armoury of food bombs to demolish the culinary oneupmanship of others. I always insist, for instance, that the *millefeuilles* at the Château de Madrid are worth negotiating the hairpin-bends of the Grand Corniche. 'I don't know why being circular should make all the difference,' I tell anyone who is listening, 'but somehow it does. Kobe beef in Tokyo is best, really, at the Hilton. They seem to have a particularly skilled masseur. You know that the Japanese massage the beasts on the hoof? I can't think why we don't do it here.'

No experience is too horrific to go into my book and be subsequently translated into a trap for the unwary.

The journey up-country from Bangkok to the Temple of Divine Light is seldom undertaken by train – at any rate by tourists, who prefer the river-steamer, or bus. I, on the other hand, went by rail, and have never forgotten the breakfast. I can still taste the cold fried egg, nestling in sago and topped with soy sauce. 'Worth all the boredom of the Jade Buddha,' I maintain, stoutly. 'Be sure and catch the nine-twenty, and insist on the restaurant-car.'

One of the legends of travel I like to retell to anyone thinking of return-ing from Australia by air and refuelling in Teheran, is that if they hasten to the Transit Lounge and take the small door on the left, next to the gentlemen's lavatory, they will find themselves at the back of the Imperial Caviare Emporium, where they have only to rouse the attendant, who sleeps under the counter, to secure enormous quantities of sturgeon roe at knock-down prices.

It may well be that the store exists, but I have not, after numerous attempts, ever discovered it. I am not sure I want to. It gives me something to look forward to on the flight.

How dull the world would be if we all knew the mystery of Glamis Castle – which reminds me of a little teashop on the left as you leave the Keep, where they serve a really excellent Scotch pancake.

Afternoon Tea Now Being Served

How perfectly Oscar Wilde understood the importance of afternoon tea. There is a line in one of his plays about the dearth of cucumbers for the sandwiches which wrings the heartstrings. 'No cucumbers, Lane?' 'Not even for ready money, sir.' I have always been devoted to afternoon tea, an afternoon without it seems purposeless, and yet quite often these days I have to go without. Not at home, of course, there is always tea at home, but without guests — and especially grandchildren — the fare tends to sparseness, and more often than not the butter has not been left out of the refrigerator. Why cannot anyone design a reasonable compartment for the butter where it doesn't freeze to death? I sometimes look at the advertisements for soft margarine and wonder whether it's worth a try. Tea, then, for what it's worth, at home is flapjacks or crumpets, shortcake and gingerbread, swiss roll and chocolate biscuits and one or two cakes which need eating up. On Sundays and feast days when we sit round the dining-room table with the family it's altogether a more elaborate affair, with ginger snaps filled with cream and playmate biscuits and cucumber and pâté sandwiches and scones and jam, and the cakes of course are fresh, like the brown bread.

Ah well, having declared my interest in tea, as they say these days, or are supposed to say, let's venture further afield and contemplate how seriously this beautiful meal is taken by the catering trade as a whole. High praise to start with to the Savoy, where I once gave a tea party to about twenty guests and was allotted a private sitting-room, two waiters and a maître d'hotel who processed around with tea and cream and milk on silver trays and offered poached eggs in muffins and five sorts of sandwiches and *millefeuilles* and chocolate cake. Just about right, and of course a butler at the tea table makes all the difference. In Kent when I was young there were Sunday teas under a cedar tree and cake stands carried in procession across the lawn and silver trays, and large cups for the gentlemen and small for the ladies. They were not my teacups or my

45

footmen, but for the rest of the week selling vacuum cleaners from doorstep to doorstep I would hug the memory of gracious living and Dundee cake.

Since the War, things have never been quite the same. Two who never survived the holocaust were Fuller's Walnut Cake and Sainsbury's Breakfast Sausage. I count myself fortunate that in my formative years, and indeed for some time afterwards, I ate my share of both. But tea shops are not what they were, particularly down South, though there is one opposite Kew Gardens which specialises in Maids-of-Honour, and Fortnum's still does its duty nobly. Indeed, their restaurant off Jermyn Street with its soda fountain is open unexpectedly late in the evenings in case you've missed out earlier, and there is deep consolation to be found in one of their elegant rarebits washed down with a chocolate milk shake.

Do my readers remember, as I do, Gunter's in Berkeley Square and Stewart's in Piccadilly, and the Trocadero in Shaftesbury Avenue? One is tempted to ask what on earth people do in the afternoon these days. Of course, there is always the Ritz.

In an endeavour to find out what happened to the trade I looked up tea shops in the Yellow Pages, to find the sole listing of such establishments is now confined to Capone, A., 38 Churton Street, S.W.1. I rang up to enquire about reserving a table, but something in my voice alerted the member of the staff who answered.

'You won't like it much here,' he told me, 'this is a tea-room for working men and we don't reserve.'

A similar enquiry to Gunter's, now in Bryanston Street, provided a more puzzling response. Tea was apparently available as long as I knew Mr. Vincent, who was out at the moment. I said I looked forward to meeting him and would it be all right if I brought a friend? The voice raised no objection and asked for the name and initial and when I'd given it, the time.

'I thought about four,' I said.

'And you're a friend of Mr. Vincent's?' Again the fatal enquiry.

'Not yet, but I hope to be a great friend after tea.'

'If you're not a friend already, I don't think you'd better come. Who are you, exactly?'

'A member of the public,' I replied with unaccustomed humility.

'We've given up entertaining them,' the voice rebuked, and hung up.

I tried Bentinck's, who used to serve tea in Bond Street and Wigmore Street, but now apparently only do so in Sloane Street, and never after five thirty. Marshall's tea is cleared away by five, as is the custom in most department stores. I feel slightly embarrassed taking tea where I am not proposing to shop or spend the night. It was not always thus. Hotels especially used to promote tea time, and Selfridge's Hotel still has a pianist. But what happened to the Gypsy Bands, what happened to the thés dansants, what happened to the trios and the quartets of gallant lady musicians who played amid the palms up and down the country from three-thirty till six, spreading a little happiness and extravagance with their repertoire of light music? 'Two teas with buttered toast, and will you ask them to play something from *Lilac Time*?' How proud, how happy I used to be when my request was granted; how appreciatively I would smile at the leader and clap all concerned. Dare I ask for the Cobbler's Song from *Chu Chin Chow* as an encore? I dared.

You will have to go a very long way indeed to recapture such pleasure, but intending travellers to Canada might care to know that in the Château Frontenac in Quebec they still strike up in the Palm Court as soon as lunch is over, and that the gentlemen of the ensemble wear wigs – not false hair pieces, you understand but genuine period wigs – tied with bows. Come to think of it, I enjoyed it more than Niagara.

Concorde and the Charing Cross Hotel

My family have always been extravagantly fond of the Charing Cross Hotel. My father used to take himself there for brief stays in moments of financial crisis, and as these were by no means infrequent, spent a good deal of time there trying to raise the wind and avoid the creditors. My sister still meets her friends there after shopping excursions from Kent, favouring the upstairs bar and tea lounge away from the commuters who crowd the downstairs ones, bracing themselves after a relaxed day at the office for the domestic encounter which has to come when the six-thirty-eight arrives, as it inevitably must, sometime, at Bexley Halt. At home there is no one to fall back upon, no secretary to iron out the crumples. At home we are all equal, each expected to pull his weight, to mend the washing machine, to speak firmly to the children, to mow the grass. Nevertheless the Charing Cross, like all London station hotels, is a cheerful place round about six-thirty in the evening: it has not perhaps the excitement of the Grosvenor at Victoria where the train to catch might just possibly not be stopping at Bognor Regis but going straight through to Budapest. Nor has it quite the 'I'm alright Jack' atmosphere of the Great Western Hotel where the drinkers tend to be large Gin and Tonics and the conversation about either the week-end just past or the one to come. If there was anything so vulgar as a polo 'crowd', these are your pucka chucka people.

No one, as far as I know, plays polo in Kent. They are far more politically minded, even at times electing Liberals. When they are not canvassing each other or voting they are carrying large trays of mushrooms down to the garden gate and selling them to passing motorists along with seasonal fruit and chicken manure. Kent is the original blackboard jungle and some of the profits find their way back to the Charing Cross Hotel. The dining-room retains the original décor, all green and pink and chaste nymphs censored from the waist down but with bust well to the fore, as might be expected of any goddess supporting a ceiling on her shoulders. There is a pianist strumming 'I Want To Be Happy' and 'Tea for Two', and a lot of space between the tables.

On the night I was there for an early dinner the customers didn't crowd each other either. Elderly couples whose lifetime habits were well known to each other: 'Madam will have a glass of Chablis – you do have it by the glass, don't you – and for myself a pint of light ale to start with.' Anything in quotes in this chapter is word for word, by the way. I have recently purchased, or to be more accurate, had lent to me with an option to purchase, a hearing aid, and I now hear perfectly what is going on around me. I can hear knives clatter, plates being scraped, people chewing, paper rustling, my own bones creaking; what I can't hear accurately is what is being said to me. Do I like the unaccustomed sounds of my own private Watergate? I am still not sure. I went to the theatre after dinner and heard every word for once, but then for once everyone spoke up.

But to return to the Charing Cross Hotel. The food was good on the whole, the melon rather old-fashioned and sliced; I disapprove of sliced melon but I suppose it's one of the first things they teach in the kitchens of the culinary schools. No doubt it makes the melon look a bit gayer, expecially when they spear a cherry and put it on the top. Gone are the days when fruit knives were made of silver, and steel was not supposed to touch fruit. My wife and I both had Wiener schnitzels. I have promised myself that for once I will be factual; there is a charm I always think in reading what the writer and his companion actually ate. When, as often happens, the new overwhelms, when cricket pitches are wilfully destroyed and no one has the courage to carry the stumps and bails a few yards and set them up on another piece of the ground, when naked men leap the wicket and row around on park ponds, when the Burtons come together again and the world holds its breath or merely lets it out in one long expiring gasp, it is comforting, surely, to read that my wife chose fruit salad and I had a chocolate éclair of immense excellence and regretted not having accepted the offer of another. We didn't order coffee but it came just the same. The bill took its time, and by then we were anxious not to miss the curtain. The pianist played 'My Heart Stood Still' as we walked out. On the whole, as it turned out, it would have been wiser to linger and let him complete his repertoire: the play was God-awful.

Hoping for once to get ahead of my colleagues, I accepted an invitation recently to fly on the Concorde all the way to Gander and back one fine summer morning and sample breakfast at twice the speed of sound and lunch at precisely the same pace. A feature of the dining-room, indeed of the cabin, is an illuminated computer sign which records the rate of sky hurtle. Whether it is the same reading as the captain takes, of course, one doesn't know for certain as you don't even pass a cloud at fifty thousand feet. The food was brisk and hot, and for breakfast there was the customary sausages, kidney, steak, mushroom, tomato and sauté potatoes, followed and preceded by champagne, a good claret, a fair white burgundy, a really delicious trifle, coffee and liqueurs.

By the time we had explored Gander – something of a ghost airport these days, alas – it was time to be thinking of getting back and luncheon. Meals will come thick and fast on the Concorde, apparently. It took two and a half hours to cross the Atlantic once more, just time for cocktails, canapés, ham stuffed with *foie gras* and supreme of chicken, excellent cheese, and fruit salad iced with brandy. The wines were the same as at breakfast. The speed seems fairly constant; either the pilot was chicken or for some reason unable to raise the speed to three times that of sound, I am not sure which. No doubt it will come.

Supersonic food will come too, and quickly; in theory there is perhaps little point in man pressing his luck but in practice he usually does.

Faced with the choice of crossing to New York in a leisurely jumbo and a chance for another look at *Gone With The Wind* and an elaborate banquet (at any rate in the first class), or a quick streak across the waves in less than half the time, I think we will all go for the streak. I don't know why; it isn't as if there was a great deal to do when we got there, but we like to think there is. There was nothing whatever to do in Gander but buy terracotta statues of Newfoundland fishermen. Even my small granddaughter, the keenest of magpies, left it behind after we had reached home for tea.

A Moveable Feast

Having spent the last month preparing a different sort of feast from those which I normally write about in my role as restaurant guide (there's no harm, surely, in mentioning that my new play opened in Birmingham last week), I haven't had the customary leisure for luncheon lately. Indeed, at the start of rehearsals, in company with my fellow players I gave up a formal meal in favour of a picnic partaken in the stalls of the empty theatre in which we were endeavouring to perfect our moves and form a nodding acquaintance with the lines. (There's one thing about being a prompter, you can't win, whether the actors pretend you've interrupted them and they were just about to utter, or whether they click their fingers in fury and shout 'Lines, please, *lines*! Isn't there *anyone* on the book?')

The picnic enchanted, alas, for approximately three days. Of course, French bread, pâté and plonk and a few cheeses are splendid once, possibly twice running, but not more. Besides, no one seemed to have the right equipment; one sighed for wicker baskets with matching thermoses, and drank out of cracked cups. After a week we feared the contagion of sordidness and lunched next door to the Cambridge at a perfectly charming club for actors, put there apparently for no other purpose than to afford us the best sausages in London, cottage pie, spare ribs and soup of the day.

I have started club life again; the atmosphere of Macready's is just right, the bar is crowded with hopeful members of my profession engaged in the class stuff. The National Theatre rehearses near by. As we hurry away to resume our practice, the voices of the Old Vic can be heard on the telephone, announcing that they are still lunching and won't be in quite at the half.

In the warmest spring weather for years (it must be spring, surely) the scent of picnics and forsythia fragrant the air. (What a poet I must have made.) In the summer I try most Sundays for the Fête Champêtre on my own lawn, constantly inspired by that advertisement for brandy which depicts the château crowd munching on the grass after the wedding. All in white except for the priest and the cognac bottle, and all one side of the table playing, like actors at rehearsals, to an invisible audience. I try to arrange my family exactly thus, although I haven't quite got either the perspective or the length of château. I haven't even got the length of table. We do our best, the grandchildren especially, but something is missing. Possibly the priest.

'There is no need to make it a picnic,' was one of the most frequent admonishments of my childhood.

My mother was wont to utter it whenever one spoon or plate was asked to do the work of two, or when the jam jar was not put back on its saucer: yet the picnic itself was in those days far from an informal affair especially when celebrated on a railway journey. The sandwiches all neatly packaged in white grease-proof had the legend of their contents clearly written in pencil. Ham and tomato, chicken and tongue paste, sardine and watercress.

One thermos contained lemonade, the other tea already milked and sugared. There was a special tin for the ginger nuts. We preferred a carriage to ourselves but if this was not possible there was still a lack of furtiveness about the feast. How sad it has always seemed to me to watch a guilt-ridden soul feeding himself from a paper bag, dipping his hand deep into the folds and fishing out some tiny morsel of sustenance to convey to his mouth with surreptitious gesture as if he hoped he would be thought to be merely coughing. There are still men today of such hideous refinement that, popping an acid drop between their gums, they give the impression that they are prisoners on remand poisoning themselves with strychnine rather than face their accusers.

Not so my family: we held up our egg sandwiches for all the world to admire and if there was any plum cake left over we would offer it around to fellow travellers. In those days the railways put up picnic baskets of their own which were ordered in advance and handed through the window at certain specified stations en route. The passenger was asked to state his preference for wing or thigh, and the bird came with ham rolls, cheese, fruit and a half bottle of wine. Passengers were on their honour to hand back the basket, or at least leave it in the carriage; any breach of trust on their part was unthinkable. Picnic baskets were usually single and in that sense not really a picnic so much as a ration. The package lunch is seldom convivial; I always sigh for those individually-packed British Directors assembled in the Albert Hall when they come to undo their little cardboard boxes and inspect the contents. Each one exactly similar to another, nothing to share, very little to swap. No cheating allowed. I remember my own field days at Wellington College when each man was supposed to fill the knapsack of the soldier in front of him with the regulation pork pie and chocolate bar. The trick, of course, was to pretend to do so – at any rate with the chocolate, the pork pies were usually filthy.

I have always enjoyed food on the move. 'Is there a restaurant car?' has been my constant enquiry and nowadays, alas, how often am I disappointed. But where it is forthcoming I can still relish the excitement with which the food on British Rail is served. Whoever is responsible for the training of our restaurant car attendants imparts his own particular flavour to the service, if not to the food. There is always an element of Mack Sennett, of the early films in the manner of the attendant – a hint of Chaplin in the walk. Then there's the speed with which plates of soup are placed before the customers: not a drop splashes over, but then there is never more than a drop to start with. The way in which the empty plates are hurled onto the table, the lightning portioning out of the slices of mutton, fair do's for all with potatoes and sprouts. Speed is the essence. One is perpetually reminded that we are all, passengers and staff alike, catching a train. In almost no time at all the meal is over, the bills distributed, the money collected, the tables cleared and we have been persuaded to return to our carriages and leave the attendants in peace. Woe betide the passenger who tries to linger – or, worse still, returns for another drink. How enjoyable a journey which didn't end when the platform arrived but lingered on in the refreshment car, a band of happy voyagers carousing till the dawn and joined perhaps by others about to start their journey, or even with no travel plans whatsoever.

Our local station has over the years been cut down to size; where there were once two tracks only a single one remains. All hints of the booking hall have been effaced – even the waiting room is usually locked.

On this deserted but tranquil scene there happened the other evening a band of youths and their girls intent on recreating that pastoral scene so seldom witnessed these days save in the Hovis advertisements on television. They took the station to be abandoned, like themselves, laid a cloth on the platform, produced cakes and ale and sat there among the midges, strumming their guitars, when suddenly the five twenty-nine commuter train from Paddington arrived with the exhausted daily breaders carrying brief-cases and umbrellas and searching their pockets for car keys. There was a confrontation, terror assailed the bowler-hat

53

brigade; they scented squatters, they remonstrated, they urged retreat. 'You won't like it here,' they told the gipsies, 'this station is used every morning by people like us trying to make a living. If you've opted out please opt out somewhere else.' But the girls and boys laughed at them. 'We are here for good,' they assured all and sundry, but in the morning they had gone.

In Switzerland, even still sometimes in France, the station restaurant is the best in town; how curious that British Rail have never understood that a station can be the focal point of a community; that every time they give up Liverpool Street to the developers or Sandhurst Halt to no one in particular they are destroying themselves. How pleasant in the evening to take a train out of the smoke, to journey down the line to some Elysian field, to find a picnic spread outside the waiting room and lobsters and champagne in the booking hall. How pleasant and how unlikely. Heigho.

As for just taking the pony cart, the *foie gras en croûte*, the cold grouse, the lobster patties, the quails in aspic, the champagne and the sherry trifle, and driving out across the heather – those days are over for most of us. The last vestige of gracious living has been banished to racecourse car parks, where one can still have one's Rolls and eat them. We indulge our national proclivity to get there and spread out now that the Empire is over and the races begin later.

The picnickers that delight me most are the lay-by layabouts, that cherished little family parked at the side of the road with a field or a heap of gravel at their back, facing the endless ribbon of cars which, unlike them, are getting on with the task in hand. Why, oh why, I ask myself, have they stopped where they have? A call of nature? A child who wants to be sick? A dog who wants to run? But not, surely, simply a meal demanding to be eaten off plastic plates? Sometimes there is a kettle boiling, sometimes an aluminium chair unfolded, always there are tomatoes. The tomato is the patron fruit of picnickers. It gives the seal of approval to the cold collation. The sort of people who pull up in lay-bys to feast are the same people who drive their cars right up to the edge of the esplanade and don't get out. For them the sea is best observed through a windscreen, the ozone let in through a half-opened window. They will not explore the sand any more than they do the turf. They have long since forgotten, if once they knew, the terror of seagulls.

When the children were younger, we used sometimes to go for river picnics, tying up the hired launch to a tree stump and squatting among the reeds, anxious always lest the boat should drift away or the engines fail to restart. But it was adventure of a sort, and for one like myself who is

54

frightened of almost all wild creatures, particularly chewing cows and running dogs, a time to muse on just how far one was prepared to go if one's loved ones were threatened by the horse grazing in the distance who might turn out to be a stallion.

The best of all picnics was once organised for me on the Island of Marmora by the champion Turkish lady sculler of her generation (how I love to drop names). We hired a caique and after a bit of bother beached on a deserted stretch of sand and swam and ate bread and butter and wild honey and figs and grapes picked in the fig groves and vineyards of an unknown farmer who, when we had finished, suddenly appeared, not to scold or demand payment, but to offer wine and a home-made liqueur. Well, Marmora was fun while it lasted, and I suppose it is just possible that I shall be picnicking again before long — on a train to Newcastle with no restaurant car but with those little labels stuck on the windows reserving our coach for 'Ghost On Tiptoe Company', and what shall we take with us — chicken sandwiches on brown bread, cucumber sandwiches heavily sugared, a pork pie, a bar of chocolate and a bottle of wine, and just possibly a corkscrew? More or less what I stuffed in my haversack fifty years ago on field days in the dreaded Officers' Training Corps.

**SUCH
STUFF
AS
DREAMS
ARE
MADE
ON ...**

Pipe Dream

'You mean to tell me,' said my neighbour, 'you have been living on top of an oil field all these years and mistook it for a vegetable garden?'

'That's right,' I told him, 'still, better late than never. They're coming with the equipment on Friday. A week, give or take, and I shall be in production.'

He asked whether it might be noisy.

'A sort of rhythmical tapping,' I told him, 'and of course a faint smell, but the gantry, I think that's what they call it, is pastel blue to match the shutters. I can give you a booklet if you like, they're the people who used to do the swimming pool, but now they've switched. Most people already have pools if they are ever going to have them. Oil is the new status symbol. They put it rather cleverly on the cover: "Rig yourself out".'

He took the literature and went back to mowing his lawn, but I could tell he was no longer concentrating. My firm, they pay for introductions.

One of the leading estate agents prints small symbols under the photographs of the houses he has for sale nowadays, designating the amenities. A horse means stabling, a dog kennelling, a diver indicates a swimming pool, there's a radiator for central heating, and now, lo and behold, a small derrick for you know what. We are keeping it pretty quiet in Berkshire, we don't want a lot of the big boys moving in, and among the crowd I go to cocktail parties with, a second derrick is considered a bit much. Three oil wells on the property and you buy your own gin and go back to dusting the mantelpiece.

Most of us sell the stuff direct and just keep back enough for the Rolls and the radiators and a little for special needs, and to give to friends. Berkshire Spirit is that much richer and visitors driving down for Sunday lunch really appreciate a special fill-up.

Our neighbourhood oil prospector was a pleasant man, dressed in the traditional costume of worn denims and tin helmet; he might have stepped straight out of the celebrated TV series. He parked his van in the drive.

'If you will just show me where the boundaries are I can get down to it,'
he explained, producing a survey map.

'Get down to what?' I asked. He looked round nervously, waited for a
load of hay to pass the gate and uttered the magic word. 'Oil. You're
loaded with it here – didn't you know?'

'I had no idea,' I told him.

'You're right in the middle of the biggest oil field between Marlow and
Sonning,' he went on, 'there's no point in taking a soil sample really, just a
formality; still, it's all part of the service. Help us site the rig; I suppose you
don't want it on the croquet lawn? Under the swimming pool, too, would
be a bit awkward, come to think of it. We'd be better in the kitchen garden,
I suppose; anyway, there's where I'll make a start, and Bob's your uncle.'

I hadn't heard anyone say 'Bob's your uncle' for a long time, but, come
to that, I'd never seen anyone prospecting for oil among the raspberries.

'I'll be a fair time,' he told me, and asked if I was planning to go out to
work. I explained that I worked at home and would be available.

'You won't have to do much more of that once we've got rigged up,' he
assured me. 'You can just sit in the shade and watch the old jigger go up
and down and every time it comes up means another bob or two in the old
pocket.' He fetched a spade and a bundle of drain rods from the back of
the lorry and marched off in the direction of the Brussels sprouts.

I don't quite know what I expected at this point; I am not even sure I
believed the fellow, but it was impossible not to admire his optimism. In
any case it was justified. About an hour later he interrupted a short piece I
was working on for a well-known travel magazine to bring me his report.

'First the good news,' he told me, 'you're stashed. I don't think I'd be far
wrong if I called if half a million barrels, give or take a couple of thousand.
Now for the bad news . . . the rhubarb will have to go. For a time I thought
we might save it but the pipe will have to come bang down the middle.'

'Forget the rhubarb,' I told him. 'We never eat it anyway.'

'I like a bit of rhubarb myself, there may be a crown or two we could
save, we'll have to see,' he went on. 'But the important thing just now is to
order the equipment and find a day to install. Would next Friday suit? I
shall be in the district, so if it's convenient for you it'll suit us both.'

I told him Friday would do admirably and asked how long the
operation would take. Apparently they'd improved the technique out of all
recognition. He reckoned, with luck, and given a fair crack of the drill, the
whole thing would be accomplished in about five hours; in six we should
be fully operational with the oil flowing, in the first instance into a static

water tank which he was letting me have second-hand and siting by the garage. Later he proposed to connect the tank by pipes to an outlet point further down the drive.

'Much the same arrangement I see you already have with fuel for the central heating system, only this time in reverse. The tankers will arrive about twice a week to start with and instead of you paying them they'll pay you and give you a receipt.'

I suggested that I might be the one to have to give the receipt but he demurred. Better not have anything in writing. 'With this Government you never know, they'll try and get a piece of it, you can count on that. They screwed those North Sea boys, and they'll crucify you if they get the chance.

'It's your land, it's your oil; I reckon you're doing them a service, making a patriotic gesture. In war-time we had to grow our own greens, now we have to grow our own oil. The only trouble, as I see it, is if we get too successful over here, we'll have another Uganda on our hands. Only this time it won't just be one wife they'll want to bring in, it'll be the whole bloody harem!

'I reckon,' he went on, 'it was a poor day for those old sheikhs when the Americans thought of Skylab. It was a poor day for America too, come to think of it. Didn't do Texas much good.'

'You mean,' I asked him, 'the Berkshire Oil Fields were spotted from Gemini?'

'Where else? That's what they were looking for. That's what they found. Anyway, you don't have to pay for that little caper, all you have to pay for is the rig and installation, and that you can do on the never-never if you wish. A cheque for a hundred pounds and your signature is all I'm asking at present, and whether you'd like the rig any particular colour. Any particular colour that's on the card, that is.'

I chose blue and wrote out the cheque to cash. I spent the rest of the day trying to find out the asking price for crude oil and how many gallons are in a barrel. That sort of information is hard to come by, unless you are in the oil game. Finally I rang Paul Getty. I met him at a party, nearly met him that is. Just as I was going to walk over to his table and say, 'Hullo, Mr. Getty, I'm Robert Morley,' he got up and left.

I wasn't more fortunate this time; apparently he doesn't care to speak on the phone, or else it's a trade secret. I made up my mind I'd have to wait until Friday.

I suppose you're thinking I was a bit of a mug; that when Friday came my neighbourhood prospector didn't turn up, and there isn't an oil rig at the bottom of my garden! I'm sorry to disappoint you. At two o'clock in the morning, if I open the window and listen, I hear, not as Kipling wrote 'the feet of the wind going to call the sun', but the tap, tap, tap, tap of the well. Twice a week a plain lorry calls to collect and hands over the cash and I now know the price of crude oil; and how many gallons to the barrel. But it's a secret. In this part of the Home Counties we don't have to discuss money, we just count it.

Our Man in Heaven

Unusually well-informed circles now consider it unlikely that Robert Morley will return to earth in the foreseeable future. The news will cause considerable disappointment to many people, especially those who had booked to see this superb artiste in future performances of *How The Other Half Loves* at the Lyric Theatre, and those who feel an even deeper concern for the future of Summitry.

It is not clear at this stage whether Mr. Morley remains an entirely free agent in the heavens, and whether his choice to remain aloft was a voluntary one. Certainly when he left last Wednesday, his avowed intention was to return to earth, but was this really so? Had he perhaps had enough, even before he started on his journey? The actor, although extravagantly well-preserved, is in his mid-sixties, traditionally at an age when the Englishman's mind turns to retirement. On the other hand, would a public performer such as himself willingly forgo the enormous publicity, and, it must be noted, the considerable financial reward, inherent in his new status as being the first man, at least in recent times, to have personally conversed with the Almighty, and got away with it? Those who witnessed his departure last week from a private airfield in the Home Counties were fearful that the journey might prove both uncomfortable and exhausting. The vehicle provided still seemed to follow the traditional lines of the fiery chariot, and although now enclosed and apparently partially jet-propelled, appeared to watchers on the ground during the first few miles of rather erratic ascent, to be turbulence-prone. Our air correspondent was frankly dismayed at the design, judging it to be considerably behind even our own Concorde. However, as he wrote at the time, it does the job and a certain austerity is to be expected. After all, God does not fling his money about. Once He has hit on a pattern, He is inclined to stick to it, at least for an age.

Besides being bereft of Mr. Morley's company, there are other implications in the new situation that has arisen. It will be remembered that a number of world leaders had, when the news of the intended departure was announced, composed personal messages of goodwill and some, including our own Prime Minister, had composed a number of questions which they wished to ask God, and which Morley had with him when he left. Morley himself was in no doubt about the topics he expected to discuss once he had recovered from the flight. In a radio interview just before lift-off, he said he was prepared to explore fully the present unsatisfactory relations between Heaven and Earth. Pollution he envisaged as being high on the agenda, and he wanted to negotiate afresh the Life Span. The formula for seventy years was, he thought, arbitrary and old-fashioned, and was palpably either too short or too long. With more years ahead in which to plan and carry out his life task, man would become more relaxed. Obviously the school leaving age could be raised substantially, but the problem of overcrowding might become more acute. On the other hand, less time – say thirty years or so – might compel man to pull up his socks. Morley did not regard it as practical or desirable to discontinue the security arrangements on this subject. On the whole, unexpected death worked well, although causing some hardship. On the question of survival after death, that was what he was going there to find out for himself, if possible, but he didn't think the information was likely to be made immediately available to man, except as was already the case among those more or less professionally interested.

Asked whom he would most wish to meet, supposing his host had planned a small reception in his honour, he supposed he would like Noah, Jonah and Potiphar included on the list. He had played the two latter on the silver screen, and had always wanted to appear as the former. He would be delighted if he were introduced to Delilah, but had a feeling he wouldn't have much in common with Samson. In any case, he pointed out, this was not a social visit, but an attempt to reach meaningful conclusions. Asked if he had thought of taking his wife, he informed us that she had had her holiday already, and found it difficult to get away at this time of the year; besides, she hadn't been asked.

Robert Morley's career on the stage has been a long and distinguished one, but it is difficult to understand why he should have been selected as an ambassador on this occasion. His playing has been almost entirely of the boulevard school, and although an occasional playwright himself and an inveterate scribbler for the press and on other people's manuscripts, he has not on the whole made any very significant contribution to the theatre. His political views were naîve to the point of insanity, and acquaintances were often appalled by the length and pointlessness of his anecdotes. Why, then, of all people did *he* get the call? We confess we are by no means sure of the answer. Admittedly he was an Englishman, a breed of which the Almighty is particularly fond, but there are a great many other Englishmen. All we can say is that in His selection, God has maintained His reputation for inscrutability. Indeed, we shall probably never know what it was exactly God was looking for.

Shangri La

The sun blazed from a cloudless sky. I leapt from the punt. 'I've forgotten my bathing trunks,' I told my father. 'I cannot bear not to bathe. You go on, and I'll meet you at the lock.' I was lucky to find a bus waiting on the grass at the river bank. Unaccountably, I failed to climb aboard, but was more successful with the next, which followed abruptly. The house was full of strangers. I was still questioning them about my swimming trunks when I awoke. I lay in the dark, suffused with disappointment, mainly, I think, because of the weather.

'While we're about it,' my subconscious told me, 'you may as well know the truth about that other dream of yours – the one when you sometimes walk along the cliff, and sometimes in the valley underneath, and always arrive at the house you never knew was there.'

'The white house?' I asked, 'with the Palladian stables?'

'That's the one.'

Shaving next morning, I wondered exactly how many times I have dreamt that particular golden dream without realising it was a dream at all, how often I have found myself bounding on the trampoline turf, gazing down at my Shangri La, and whether I shall ever get there again.

Colour on the television screen, for me, makes even wild life bearable, however impatient I feel at the efforts of the white hunter to drug the hippopotamus with a poisoned dart and carry him off unprotesting to other pastures; however weary I am of watching giant tortoises plodding around the Seychelle Islands, the fact that the sun is shining, and the sky is blue – provided I have adjusted the set correctly – makes the whole thing just, but only just bearable. I long, of course, for the hunter to be hoist with his own petard, for the shot of him helplessly trussed in a net, being lowered onto Wimbledon Common from a helicopter piloted by an enormous chimpanzee. But so far there has been no significant breakthrough in this direction. I have never yearned for the veldt. I am not in essence a great open space man, but the idea of 'instant safari' proved irresistible, when I recently had a morning to kill near Bath. From the moment I read the A.A. signs so generously displayed, 'The Lions of Longleat', I found my pulse quickening. I even turned off the radio, the better to concentrate, as I gazed out across the fields and reminded myself I was in lion country. The precautions to guard the visitors, and no doubt the even more valuable lions, strike a delicate balance between apprehension and reassurance. The high wire gates are operated with extreme caution by white hunters with rifles at the ready. Moreover, two sets of them ensure that even if a lion penetrated the first defence, he would be held incommunicado in a steel meshed lock.

The lions, on the day I visited them, lay on their backs, their paws extended to the sun. Black and white Jeeps were parked beside the prides, in each a white hunter sat, tense, expectant, never taking his eyes from the passing motorists. Every now and then from the loudspeakers in the treetops came the warning to wind up windows. I left the Reserve with a feeling of immense satisfaction. Not only had the whole thing gone without a hitch, and I had been as close to a lion as I should ever want to be, but I must have saved at least a thousand pounds. It is difficult to know what effect sanctions are having in Rhodesia, but Lord Bath must be costing South Africa a fortune.

The tour of Longleat itself was something of an anti-climax, despite the efforts of a splendid guide. I am something of a connoisseur of guides, and I must award this one a very high rating indeed, if only for the way he tactfully withdrew attention from his Lordship's more recent photographic efforts. But then, I suppose I am not an easy man to please, and the huge dining-room table, laid for guests who will never be invited, recalled the Hearst Ranch in California, where only the ketchup bottles on the refectory table still serve to remind us of how awful the food and company must have been. Here at Longleat the salt cellars are panniers carried on the back of silver donkeys. If there's one thing I collect, it is silver donkeys. For an instant I wondered if they would be missed. Not as much as the lions, I'll be bound.

I have a childlike faith in my own ability to get things done, which is why I went in person to the Chinese Consulate to demand a visa. I can't pretend I got off to a flying start, and couldn't decide whether, as I waited in the hall, I was interviewed by the same man three times, or three different men once. When they all look alike it doesn't really help for them all to dress alike. It was pointed out to me that owing to the behaviour of the British Government, 'un-normal relations' existed between our people and theirs. There was no hope at all of any further exchange of visitors this year. Next year perhaps – meanwhile they suggested I should write to the Chinese Tourist Centre in Peking. I told them I didn't fancy my chances of getting an answer, and enquired how long it would take for my letter to reach Peking. Two days, I was informed. Posted in London? Posted anywhere in England, *two* days. They shrugged off my disbelief, courteously refused my handshake, and showed me the door. I no longer believe war with China to be quite such a remote possibility as I used. A nation which can be unrealistic about Global Postage might be equally so about Global Warfare.

Folie de Grandeur

I am a Minister, but not of the Church. I sit in an enormous office at an enormous desk and am enormously occupied. It is enormously difficult to see me. Appointments have to be made months ahead.

I have got much thinner and am now beautifully dressed. I have two private secretaries, one young, the other not so young. They are both dedicated to serving me. Simpkins would give his life for me. Matthews will do just that, but doesn't know it yet.

The pictures are my own – two Rembrandts and a Manet. Only I would dare hang them on the same wall. When I go I shall take them with me, but that will not be for a long time. Meanwhile there is work to be done.

I never speak on the 'phone. My decisions are always final. They are written in a hand I would not have recognised as mine when I came here first. My visitors know my time is precious: they seldom stay more than a few moments. I listen (something I have learnt to do) and occasionally interject a sentence or two. I stand to signal that the audience is at an end, and my guests leave, refurbished utterly from head to toe, their faces glow, they walk backwards. Backwards? Am I the Pope? Royalty? The Aga Khan? Not the Pope certainly, nor the Aga Khan. There can't be all that pressure in Sardinia, even though he's married. Am I getting married? Am I married already?

There is a private apartment somewhere, but my family life is a closed book. I am not certain whether I'm married or not. If I have children they're 'Spanish type'. They are exactly the right number, the right sex and the right age. We are to be seen dining en famille at the Ritz, flexing in beach cabanas, playing touch football. We refused a fortune to be photographed advertising brandy en plein air. Are there ten, fifteen, seven of us? It depends on what we are doing. Sometimes we play chess, and then of course we are two. The one behind, bringing the coffee, is the footman.

Preparing a few personal notes about myself, at the request of some learned foundation or other, I described myself as an adequate man. *The* adequate man perhaps would have been more honest. I have never met another. I am always hoping to. Every time the doors open at the end of the room, and I rise to meet another stranger, I search his face for a sign that he too is adequate, and will be ready to share my burden. How heavy this burden is, I can never exactly find out. I am tired, naturally, but by now resigned to fatigue. When I smile it is as if the sun shines. When I furrow my brow in displeasure, people have remarked that it actually gets darker.

I have one of those watches that can be worn on the high diving-board, not that I dive often these days, there simply isn't the time.

Simpkins has just come in with some papers for me to sign. I have just decided to make it mandatory for motorists to drive a minimum of eight miles on every occasion they exercise their cars. Neither they nor their passengers must alight from the vehicle until an hour or more has elapsed from the moment of entry. I have solved traffic congestion, but Simpkins was not pleased. He lives in Highgate and prides himself on doing the journey in fifteen minutes. From now on he will have to drive to the Alexandra Palace, wait thirty minutes in his motor, and walk back. If he parks his car correctly, the journey here in the mornings will present no problems as long as he leaves forty minutes earlier. The curious thing is that I am practically certain I am not the Minister of Transport, but Simpkins seemed to find nothing unusual in my demand. Possibly I am Minister without Portfolio, charged with special tasks.

I have decided to return Gibraltar to Spain forthwith. I can see no point in retaining it any longer, and it's not as if I ever intended to go there. Of course this is not my only reason. I plan later this year to summon King Juan Carlos, the Generalissimo's successor, to London. I am almost certain that is where I still am. I am going to demand that he accepts my offer to run tourism in Britain. When he has had time to grade our hotels and hang up those price lists in the closets, we can make ready for influxes of Spanish day trippers at Lords. It will be the salvation of cricket.

Simpkins has just come in to ask how he will know when he has been in his car for an hour, as he has broken his watch. After next month, cars will be fitted with time locks. There is no problem but the problem itself, I tell him. (One for the book, I fancy.)

My plan for the compulsory retirement of all workers at forty seems to be working well. Speeding up the rat race makes it a spectator's sport. After sixty, spectators are free to get back into harness. They can apply to be taken on as traffic wardens, night watchmen, domestic or civil servants.

Promotion in all walks of life is rapid. If a boy hasn't got it made at seventeen, there's not much hope for him. The average age of bank managers in this country is now nineteen; doctors can qualify three years earlier.

On my seventieth birthday I shall definitely give up the editorship of *Punch*. It is extraordinary how I have been able to combine it with my other activities all these years. In some ways it is the least arduous of my tasks. One merely sets the subject of the essay and leaves the rest to the hacks. I shall probably appoint a schoolmaster to succeed me.

Simpkins and Matthews are back. It seems it is time for my tea. I wonder why they persist in wearing white.

BÊTES
NOIRES

What Salvation Army?

On some Sunday mornings, a car will stop at the gate and an old lady, mysteriously ejected, will trudge up the drive and ring my bell. When I open the door, she allows no flicker of recognition. As far as she is concerned apparently, we have never met before. She starts straight in on her pitch for God. She is what they call a Jehovah's Witness, and because she has walked up the drive, and because I suspect her ankles are troubling her, and perhaps because it's Sunday and I am aware of ancient taboos, I let her carry on for a while before I tell her that this is not a Christian settlement and although the tribes that live here are friendly, they are incapable of being converted. 'Go in peace,' I tell her, and firmly and inhospitably close the door, because if I don't, she'll be there forever. Mysteriously, the car is now no longer in evidence. I don't know what happens when she reaches the gate. She might, for all I know, ascend at once to heaven, and surely on those ankles she can't get far. But I like to think as she walks down the drive that she's in better shape for having encountered such a noble savage as myself. Evangelists nowadays come in all shapes and sizes; only the humble I find tolerable.

I have a friend whose son, like Malcolm Muggeridge, stumbled on God. She is not pleased. Was the Virgin Mary similarly harrassed and dismayed? Did Christ come home at weekends with the laundry, and did He behave like her child does, enjoying the cooking and upbraiding the guests? What sort of baby was Christ? What sort of child? My friend's son, whom I have known all his life, gave no hint of the trouble to come until he was at least thirty. In his youth it was I who gave the advice. 'Promise me you will never go on the stage,' I urged. And when one day he left the biscuit counter at Fortnum & Mason's to take up acting, and became a film star overnight, he never reproached me for my advice. Those times are past. Now he cleans telephones with evangelical pride. He earns his bread the hard way. We don't meet often, and when we do he constantly struggles to save my soul, even before he has ordered the food.

'Every word is true, Uncle Mor,' he insists. 'Although you may not choose to believe it, there is literally a lake of fire, and if you don't look out, that's where you'll find yourself.'

'But surely,' I tell him, 'it won't matter.'

'Won't matter?' He has picked up the menu now and peers at me over the top of it. 'It will be very uncomfortable.'

'But,' I tell him, 'I shall be a spirit. I shan't feel any pain. I'm not supposed to keep my body, or am I?'

For some reason he evades the question. 'If you don't mind,' he remarks, 'I think I'll start with the smoked salmon.'

That's what gets his mother down, and me for that matter, when I'm paying. He should be living on curds and whey, and so, come to think of it, should Muggeridge. It's monstrous the way Muggeridge always has the best chair in the studio, and the best suit and tie. Very often he's the only one with a tie. He's always so much better shod than the Franciscan monk or the protest leader or the permanent agnostic.

But it's his bland assumption, shared by my friend's son, that he has been saved and I haven't, that absolutely infuriates me. What makes Muggeridge so special? He lives exactly like the rest of us. I once saw him driving down the King's Road. He didn't look as if he was praying. There was a terrible series on the television called 'Muggeridge in the Steps of Saint Paul'. Muggeridge and his friend, who seemed to be a sort of superior courier and was obviously boned-up on the Dead Sea Scrolls, or some such trivia, kept getting themselves stuck in crypts and photographed leaning nonchalantly on reredoses, and all I could think of were the sweating electricians and the exhausted boom boys and the red-eyed cameramen who had patiently tracked these elderly mountain goats on their awful picnic, who had followed them across the sand dunes and along the tracks, humping their equipment and recording the platitudes. Around the rugged rocks these ragged rascals rant, and oh God, the boredom and effort involved, and the insufferable superiority of the twain.

It's sad to think that years ago Muggeridge was quite a gay dog, and what is even rarer, a witty gay dog. The wit and the gaiety have left him. All that remains is John the Muggeridge crying, not, alas, in the wilderness where at least no one would hear him, but on the box. Like Herod, I too am irritated and would not, were I pressed, be able to resist presenting his head to Joan Bakewell. I cannot forgive the awful hypocrisy of his asking 'Why?' Why sex? Why Government? Why pollution? Why masturbation? The man is incapable of listening to the answer for more than a minute without interrupting and contradicting his informant. He doesn't want to be told, he wants to tell. We may or may not deserve the wrath to come, but what have we done to deserve such a missionary?

City Bluff

When people start telling me what exactly is the trouble with this land of ours I find myself looking round desperately for my hat. I know already they will postulate the theory that no one wants to work anymore except presumably (as judgement is always passed with more than a hint of disapproval) themselves.

Those who are so anxious to condemn their fellow citizens, as if not wanting to work is a vice and not a virtue, are nearly always holding a glass or scraping their plates after a hearty meal. Alternatively they are leaning out of car windows surveying the British worker enjoying his tea break, preparing himself for another tussle with the macadam, another spell with the giant caterpillar.

No one enjoys an argument more than I but on this subject, I cannot trust myself to speak patiently enough to be understood. How does the cretin, I ask myself silently, imagine he got here in the first place? I don't mean to just the party where he may or may not have been conveyed by some vehicle manufactured, and possibly even driven by his fellows, but out of his mother's womb? From the moment when he occasioned his parent her first labour pain he has been giving trouble, causing others to shift for him, and he will go on doing so until the last nail has been driven into his coffin, men have sweated to bury him in the ground or burn him in the fiery furnace, and the clergyman has had all the trouble first to learn to read and then to pass the requisite examinations to be permitted to read the burial service over him.

I have never met a stockbroker who didn't assure me over the second martini that he worked a great deal harder than a miner, or a banker who didn't claim to put in longer hours. Bluff is the stock-in-trade of the square mile which encloses the Mansion House. 'But the City has nothing on at all,' said a little child. 'Listen to the voice of innocence,' exclaimed his father, and what the child had said was whispered from one to another. 'But he has nothing on at all,' at last cried out all the people. The City was vexed for it knew that the people were right, but thought the procession must go on now. And the Lords of the Bedchamber took greater pains than ever to appear to be holding up invisible exports, although in reality there were no invisible exports to hold up.

They bluff their way, these City gents. They dress themselves up in jabots and furbelows and pretend to be Worshipful Fishmongers or Worshipful Bowyers when they've never cast a line or shot an arrow, and don't intend to. They have a compulsion to pass judgement. If they can't climb on the bench they will hoist themselves onto political platforms or pre-empt a chair on a television chat show, to criticise and admonish and warn and threaten. They have nagged and bitched at the public for longer than I can remember. They are constantly at panic stations, the wind cooling their broth, the sand in the hour glass enough to frighten them out of their senses, if they had any. Millions are wiped off the shares one day, millions put on the next. Every time the market moves, the City makes a killing, and what it kills is confidence in the honesty and probity of a system where a man can make a million between luncheon and tea and never pick up anything heavier than a telephone. 'How is it done?' we ask, enviously, 'how do they get away with it?', and when, as usually happens, they cry all the way back from the bank where they have stacked the bread, that we are lazy, indolent and thoroughly bolshie, we marvel at their impertinence and ask each other how long, oh Lord?

The answer is quite a long time. I expect the City to be dressing itself up in fur-lined pinafores and funny hats and sitting down to banquets for years and years to come. We are not a people eager for revolution, we do not want the blood to flow, though a little blood-letting might lower the pressure. We expect to have the rich, like the poor, with us for a long time to come, but I think we would like them to acknowledge that all their talk and advice on the economy, and their continual admonishment to the rest of us to pull up our socks is for them a part-time exercise, and what really concerns them and occupies their working and indeed waking hours is the acquisition of personal wealth. Every time they pretend otherwise they aim a brick straight through their own precious glass house.

What I suppose the rest of us would ask, if it's impossible for them to shut up, is that they should go away to Luxembourg or Monte Carlo and remove the bottle neck which bars our way to the Essex coast, or if this is not possible, couldn't we get them to take a leaf out of the dear late Margaret Rutherford's film *Passport to Pimlico*, and opt out of a country the inhabitants of which they now so obviously dislike and despise?

In time the rest of us might be quite pleased to visit them on package tours to witness their quaint old customs and admire their centuries-old costumes and to watch them stuffing themselves at banquets; we might even help them to pass round the loving cup once again.

The Case Against Conservation

Whatever happened to the pink-footed geese, the ones Peter Scott used to chase after on that tiny Arctic pony of his? I never knew where my sympathies were supposed to lie, all three seemed to be having such a terrible time. In the end someone wrote to *The Times* and said the geese didn't really care for it, and in the process the young ones got separated from their parents and died of fright. I kept waiting for Scott to write back to defend the birds' right to wear one of his patent foot tags, but as far as I know he never did. Nowadays you see his tag mostly on knitwear.

I hope Mr. Scott won't think this is a personal attack on him on behalf of the geese. I couldn't care less if I never saw a pink-footed goose again, indeed I am not even sure I have ever seen one. True, there are geese living on the river bank at Henley, and I like watching them at dusk, circling the supermarket, very pretty and squawky and in a way threatening, but I doubt they're pink-footed, just muddied.

On the other hand I am always seeing Peter Scott on the box – the Kenneth Clark of the Marshes. I even once took tea with him at the Wildfowl Trust, but there didn't seem many wildfowl about, or trust either, come to that. The birds crouched against the imprisoning wire netting. Some of them, indeed, seemed to be missing a few wing feathers. They seemed extravagantly listless.

I suppose it's all part of 'Civilisation'. The children come to see the black-tailed godwit, just as they flood in to see Tutankhamun's death mask. Once they have glimpsed it, they don't have to bother again. Off to the salt mines with them, they had their chance.

How awful, claim the conservationists, if the child never saw a dead Egyptian or an okapi or even a butterfly. We must set to work and make sure they do. The first thing to do is raise the ready. No conservationist ever admits to needing money to conserve himself, but of course there are things he simply must have – helicopters and poisoned darts, landrovers and rhinoceros nets, recording equipment and cameras and miles and miles of film stock. The cinema industry started to decline when it was discovered that all the world needed to satisfy the demand of its customers was roughly one hundred and fifty feature films a year. Up to then they had been making an average of five thousand. Similarly, if no one ever again photographed a lion, there would still be sufficient shots of lions to last the human race for another six hundred thousand years. (The statistics in this chapter are entirely my own invention.) There is, luckily, absolutely no chance of the human race lasting that long. In our case, as in every other case, the conservationists are fighting Mother Nature, and no one ever gets the better of her for long, but it doesn't stop them trying.

Once they have kitted themselves and their friends out and booked the air freight space, they are off on their lugubrious task of counting the puff adders or upturning the giant tortoises, and back before you can say David Attenborough to record the commentary and book prime time on BBC 2. They know that the rest of us have little if any chance of ever making the trip ourselves. We shall never feel the sun on our backs or smell the frangipani leis or drink guava juice. We shall not bathe on warm beaches or eat fresh coconuts, fly over the volcano or shoot the rapids. We shall live out our proscribed lives in the shadow of South Kensington Underground Station. 'Don't worry,' Peter Scott tells us, 'just put up the money and we will bring you back the colour transparencies. Hold them up to the light bulb and you will swear you, too, are standing in the Gobi Desert.'

What right have these people to represent us on these junkets? Who appointed them our ambassadors of pleasure? Is it on our instructions that they bundle up a drugged rhinoceros and move him thousands of miles up country or down country? 'He'll be happier now,' they tell us, 'and wasn't it exciting when he nearly impaled old Fred on his horn? Did you know that rhinoceros horn is widely regarded by the Chinese as an aphrodisiac? That's why we have to keep moving this one around.' 'We do know,' we shout back to the unheeding box. 'You've told us a thousand times, and now we have news for you. Rhinoceros horn is an aphrodisiac. That's why the Chinese don't need conservationists.'

If Peter Scott never drew another flying duck, if he opened all the cages and set the geese free, and if he never conducted another package tour to wrap up the penguins or stopped telling me that if something isn't done soon there will be no more white leopards around, I should be so grateful I'd even buy one of his sweaters, supposing I could find one to fit me.

But what, you ask, is the poor fellow to do in future? Well, here's one suggestion. Collect some money, buy a shooting truck and some poisoned darts – the ones that put the rhinoceros to sleep, but not so strong this time – and creep up one night to Notting Hill Gate and capture a little family of human beings living in the dried-up waterbed in Ladbroke Grove, put them on board and set them free in clean new quarters in Windsor Great Park. The game warden is his old friend and patron, H.R.H., so that should be all right.

Why Can't the North Be More Like Me?

When I was a touring actor there were some dates which struck terror in my feeble heart – Rochdale, Oldham and Darlington. I don't know whether Darlington's changed much. It didn't seem to have done the other morning, when I glimpsed it from the railway track, but my heart certainly hasn't. Every man has his particular Hell, and for years I have been preserving mine. 'How would you like,' I tell myself, 'to be stuck forever in a faceless street in the north of England, with only good neighbours for company?' I should hate it. The northerners' hearts may beat warmer than southern ones, but the real difference between us is that northerners put up with things which we southerners wouldn't. They put up with ugliness and gloom, their buildings have a positive tradition of grime and neglect. Any shed is good enough to house a railway engine. It doesn't matter that it's made of tin and rusty, and half falling down. Eyesores are acceptable north of Welwyn Garden City.

It's not only what the northerners put up that worries me, it's what they leave lying around. They are so untidy. They go out of their way to make the worst of themselves. I know I am sticking my neck out, but sometimes even elderly tortoises such as I have to stick their necks out, have to plod up the A1 and see what's happening the other side of the fence.

On just such a journey to Durham last winter, I chose the day when the snow fell. I was as surprised as everyone else to gaze out and see beautiful Berkshire covered with the stuff. I started off up the M4 in the general direction of Durham, and after an hour's crawl, reached the airport. I hadn't intended to fly, but I couldn't see much chance of getting there any other way. At Heathrow no one seemed to know what had hit them. 'It's snow,' I told the girls at the enquiry desk. 'Someone will have to sweep it off the runways.' 'No good doing that while it's still snowing,' they told me. 'In any case, there's an industrial dispute.' They cancelled the flight to Newcastle as soon as I bought my ticket, but everyone agreed there was a good chance later, if the aeroplane which was still waiting at Newcastle could be persuaded to take off from there. They rang Newcastle, but nobody seemed to want to commit themselves. 'Better to be safe than sorry,' I told myself, and if the worst came to the worst I mightn't have to go north at all. I should simply telephone Durham University, where I was due to speak, and point out it wasn't my fault. Meanwhile I sat tight. Every now and then the Director General of Civil Aviation, Heathrow, addressed us personally through the loudspeaker. He kept apologising for the weather and for the strike.

About lunchtime we were urged to proceed through Gate No. 1 and after waiting the customary ten minutes for the bus, were stowed inside the plane, fastened our seatbelts and listened to a short speech, by the pilot this time, in which he expressed the customary good wishes and gratitude for our patronage, and announced a delay of an hour before we were airborne. For some reason this produced an absolute storm of protest from the passengers. Why, they demanded, had they been strapped in, and what about dinner? The business babies among us banged their mugs on their plastic trays and screamed for Nanny. Nanny came, and handed out biscuits, and after a certain amount of tantrums, gin and tonics. She gave us clearly to understand that she was not pleased with her charges, and it was not the policy in the nursery to serve drinks on the ground.

When we got to Newcastle at a quarter to three, I fell straight into the cleverly arranged booby-trap. The restaurant, although still full of diners, had closed ten minutes earlier. I was directed to the cafeteria, where I ate two poached eggs and a chocolate biscuit, reading the social diary in a glossy to keep up my spirits and try to pretend I hadn't arrived after all.

The hotel in Durham had a plaque boasting that it had been there when Oliver Cromwell arrived, a fact which interested me a good deal less than the immediate awareness that it was not centrally heated. However, to be fair – and we southerners do try to be fair to the north – there was a very jolly chambermaid, who made me welcome, turned on a small electric fire in the bedroom and enquired whether I would like a hot water bottle. I thanked her for the offer, and was assured that she would put the bottle in the bed last thing before she went off duty. 'When will that be?' I asked, and she indicated round about five-thirty. At six, when I left the hotel, clergymen were streaming out of the dining-room and off to bed, no doubt before their bottles cooled. On the river, men were rowing, snow settling momentarily on their oars.

I was delighted, when I arrived at the Union, to find that the noble lord who had earlier promised to refute me in debate, had chickened out because of the weather. 'I found no difficulty in getting here,' I lied, and subsequently dazzled the students with a display of verbal fireworks – or did I? To be quite honest, I was a bit disappointed by both of us. I am used to being disappointed by myself, but the students were so tremendously un-trendy. One of the girls even brought her knitting. The speeches were mild and unexceptional. Files, sit-ins, demonstrations, student unrest, were not topics about which they wished to comment, or indeed to listen. Six out of six whom I quizzed later, over cider and sandwiches, were determined to vote conservative at the next election.

'I simply don't understand you,' I told them. 'It's so different where I come from.'

'Where do you come from?' they asked.

'The south.'

'That's where we come from too.' Few Durham students, I learnt, are Geordies.

In the morning I found they had rebuilt Durham Railway Station, or were planning to do so. That's the impression one gets from the north, there's always a plan – a plan to rebuild the hotel, widen the main street, knock down the old terrace house. There's a plan to clean up the Town Hall, a plan to build a theatre, modernise the hospital. 'Patience,' the north counsels. 'Rome wasn't built in a day.' Alas, it's not Rome we're considering, but Darlington. Perhaps I'm short of patience. I expected to be able to buy a newspaper on Durham Station. I expected a seat in the waiting-room. I even expected the railway carriage to be heated, and so it was – once we got to Hitchin.

I Could Have Danced All Night

'This dance,' Mr. Durrell assured me, 'is native to the village. It is performed nowhere else on the Island.'

'I don't wonder,' I replied.

'I hope,' my companion went on, 'you are not thinking of buying a house; there are far too many of us here already.'

I reassured him. If anything would decide me not to settle permanently in Corfu it would be the spectacle of three elderly crones, arms linked and ankles swollen in unison, stirring the dust. Not a good mover myself, I am jealous of the leaping crowd. Not that these ladies leaped, they shuffled. Shuffling is the fashion abroad. Sitting in the sunshine in Capri last summer, the whole square erupted with conga madness. One moment the British were chewing their olives and the next they had snaked off down the water's edge and hopefully, as far as I was concerned, into it, crazed and dishonest lemmings, leaving their campari bills unsettled. Ten minutes later an aged and solitary Member of Parliament returned in the manner in which he had departed, two steps forward and one back, but now with no girlish bosom on which to rest his elbow.

'Not dancing, Morley?' the fellow enquired, helping himself to my frozen daquiri. 'In Capri everyone dances.'

'I don't,' I told him.

I believe the Monarch shares my inhibition. I catch her sometimes on my television screen, sitting curiously upright and tensed in the green canvas chair under the palm tree, surveying her own, or nowadays, alas, more often other people's subjects, prancing around the totem pole. Do we, I wonder, feel the same about ballet when we are obliged to watch it? Is she, too, miles ahead, as I am, of the programmed scenario, optimistically but mistakenly believing we are past the wedding rites and approaching the final pirouette, only to discover that what we took for the marriage ceremony was merely the rape of the temple dancers and that there is at least another bad twenty minutes to go?

Why am I always so impatient for the dance to end? Is it because as a child I was taken by my father to so many musical comedies when all I longed for was to see a play? I sat hunched with boredom, watching the orchestra pit for the moment when the occupants would submerge and I could be sure of at least a few moments of plot or comic relief. How quickly the magic moments flew by until the dreaded musicians began groping their way back again, the conductor resumed his seat and tapped with his baton, and some fool spoilt *The Maid of the Mountains* for me by bursting into song and prance.

Or is it simply because I was never able to dance myself? In adolescence I tried to learn. I took ballroom dancing lessons from a Miss Peeler in the very best part of Pimlico; at least I took one from her and the rest from her assistants. The day Miss Peeler personally intervened is one I shall always remember. At first I mistook her interest in me for admiration; she rarely taught the beginners herself. She must, I thought, have discerned some hidden talent in me and was anxious to exploit it. There was a slight hesitancy on the part of my regular teacher when she announced that Miss Peeler herself desired to hold me in her arms and we were to go to the main ballroom, where we found the headmistress all in black with a rather more superior gramophone than the other studios boasted, and eager to commence. We took a few steps around the floor and stopped abruptly. Miss Peeler spoke, and I realised her role on this occasion was not that of a talent scout, but of a trouble-shooter.

'I didn't believe it,' she told me, 'and I wanted to see for myself, but, Mr. Morley, I wish you to know that for you I am breaking a lifelong rule and returning your fee in full. I have only done it once before in thirty years. You will never learn to dance.'

It was a snap judgement which has not been reversed. True, I later comported (if that is the word, and I fancy it is), comported myself in a musical comedy at Drury Lane believing, wrongly as it turned out, that anything Rex Harrison could do, I could do better, but my reason for accepting the engagement was not so much to prove Miss Peeler wrong after all those years as to enjoy myself at someone else's expense (considerable, as it turned out). At last, I told myself as I signed the contract, I shall see a bit of life as it should be lived backstage. I can only report that dancers are not the romantic crowd they are made out to be. Backache, not heartache was the sole topic of conversation in the wings, unless we happened to be joined by the singers, in which case we discussed tonsilitis.

But to return to the global scene and to the dancing girls and boys who were once the prerogative of emperors, but are now to be found supplementing the table d'hôte of resort hotels from Kenya to Katmandu. 'The Commodore proudly presents its troop of genuine native dancers,' announces the bandleader, and out from the service entrance trip the proud creatures themselves, arrayed in traditional plastic to re-enact with remarkable detachment the ritual stomp preceding a long-since discontinued, and indeed in their case never actually sampled, cannibal feast. Not a missionary to be seen, but alas, a certain number of pots, my own included. At least Her Majesty is not expected to participate when, their performance concluded, they invite us to rise from our chairs and join them in a simplified version of the Hula Hula or Beri Beri. This is when I put on my bravest face and indicate as best I can in local miming slang that I have a wooden leg. I shake my head and smile until the danger has passed and some other idiot is hopping in my stead, blissfully aware that it is all included in the cover charge. He may even be hoping to strike up some form of rapprochement with his coy partner, little realising that long before midnight has struck she will be off once more through the service hatch in a puff of steam to climb into the minibus at the staff entrance and on to her next engagement.

How perfectly Lewis Carroll anticipated the advent of the dancing tourist:

> 'Will you walk a little faster?' said a whiting to a snail,
> 'There's a porpoise close behind us, and he's treading on my tail.
> 'See how eagerly the lobsters and the turtles all advance,
> 'They are waiting on the shingle. Will you come and join the dance?
> 'Will you, won't you, will you, won't you, will you join the dance?
> 'Will you, won't you, will you, won't you, will you join the dance?
> 'You can really have no notion how delightful it will be,
> When they take us up and throw us with the lobsters out to sea.'

I wish I had had the wit to quote him to Lawrence Durrell as we sat in the taverna, waiting for our stuffed vine leaves, while the staff, arms linked with the visitors in suspect bonhomie, imitated a drooping line of aged Tiller girls, and to hell with the service.

Down with the Preservationists!

There are few people I find myself more often in profound disagreement with than John Betjeman. He is forever discovering the beauty in the eye of the beholder, extolling the tile-work of a public lavatory in Bootle. I dread Bootle. Most of all I dread being caught short in Bootle. One of Betjeman's recent campaigns concerned the preservation of the Criterion Theatre, another underground building famous for its ceramics. Personally, like the Brighton Belle, I should not mourn its passing. A most uncomfortable train, a most uncomfortable theatre – that is if you hate stairs, as I do. Ave atque vale! Ave atque vale, Betjeman, too!

I know such sentiments may shock the reader. John Betjeman is a good thing. Property developers are a bad thing. It's as simple as that. Property developers seldom write poems. They are not often photographed in floppy hats on Euston Station. When their photographs do appear in the papers, they do not reassure; hard-bitten men, signally lacking in charisma, whereas Betjeman is soft, cuddly, the sort of chap you could warm your feet on. He goes to church, if not to pray, at least to explain to the rest of us how important it is to recognise a Norman tower.

Did we create Betjeman, or did he create us, the silent majority who approve of the olde order, who already have our houses in the green, green belt, who chortle over the plight of those who wish to join us? A caravan site, a housing estate, a council cottage, these are bad things. A forge, an oast house, a castle, a cathedral, these are good things. We are nice people, not quite as nice as Betjeman perhaps, but nice enough. We simply cannot understand why people should want to spoil the field next door by coming to live there. We acknowledge the need for new houses; indeed, if we are fortunate enough to have land on which building restrictions can be lifted, or seem as if they might be lifted one day, we are not averse to selling it for a packet, explaining to our friends that we simply had to see little Edward through Harrow.

But on the whole we resist by all the means at our disposal anyone else coming within a mile of us – to live, that is. 'You are lucky,' my friends tell me, 'what's the secret?' 'Double Green Belt,' I tell them, preening. 'It's as simple as that.' At the bottom of the road, a mile away, the Belt stops abruptly, the houses jostle one another. The proud owners have the worst of both worlds as they sit in their little gardens, gazing at their neighbour's garage. They do it for the children, of course.

Most children hate the country. When I was young, nothing bored me more than walking in the country; walking in towns was a different matter altogether. Happily I trudged the streets, peering into strangers' faces, each one a new delight, a new surprise. I gazed into a shop window as if into Aladdin's Cave, and when at weekends I was banished to Kent, surely the dullest of all counties, I fretted with boredom, glowered at the chickens with displeasure, hated the cows. What madness pervades Betjeman, that he can be content to stare at the steeple and browse among thatched cottages in some stagnant backwater of England? What excites me is not land, but living. I would that every man was allowed to live where he liked and how he liked, and if I had it in my power I would grant Betjeman the gift of living when he likes, and banish him to the Victorian era which he professes to admire. For the rest of us, I would decree that a man may build as he chooses, and where he chooses, a shack, a bungalow, a castle, a cathedral if he has the money, and is so inclined. I would give him squatters' rights in all the broad acres. He could even come and build in my wood, if he chose. I do not believe that human beings spoil the land by living on it, quite the reverse. If a man wants to live on his own, let him. If he wants to live in a cluster, let him. If he wants to live like a pig, let him. But most men do not want to live like pigs. They are as house-proud as badgers, forever striving to improve their set. Like badgers too, their time is brief, there is no proof it comes again.

There is nothing more boring than the elegant formality of ordered living, nothing more heartening than the chaos of people and children, even dogs. Let us give back to the English the belief that their home is their castle, and that they are entitled to build it where and as they please. It may not always look like a castle; it will never please Betjeman. Buildings, like men, crumble to dust, and when the last of us have slipped away and the children have stopped playing, and no one is untidy any more, and the silence is total, then and only then let us give the country back to the woodpigeons and the butterflies and to old, old, old, old Mr. Betjeman himself.

Death to the Flannelled Fools

I have a friend, W. Rushton, an actor like myself, a creature of the dusk who earns his living lampooning Prime Ministers on the Box. I came upon him the other afternoon in a meadow, dressed all in white, a forlorn uneasy moth of a fellow unaccustomed to the daylight and in boots which seemed to be causing him discomfort. He was, he affirmed, playing cricket for money: the fact that he wasn't going to get the money himself didn't seem to disturb him as it surely would have done on a more normal occasion.

Living as I do in Berkshire, I am used to oak trees displaying posters advertising charity cricket matches – indeed am grateful for the warning not to approach too closely on such occasions – but Rushton, not for the first time, had caught me unawares. I withdrew hastily. I would rather watch a man at his toilet than on a cricket field, but such is the madness of the players that in time they come to believe that the spectacle they make of themselves dressed in white wielding a willow (to use their own revolting phraseology – and why not?) is something their betters should pay to see.

'Car Park two shillings,' the posters proclaim. 'All proceeds to H.R.H. Duke of Edinburgh', and blow me if the public don't drive their cars through the gate over the cart tracks, park in the cow dung, wind down the windows, turn up the radio and tell each other that they are getting a bit of fresh air.

It is not, of course, everybody who rolls up on these occasions, mostly people who still have drawing-rooms and take the *Telegraph* and *Punch* and who, like myself, were brought up in the shadow of The Awful Game.

I have never got over the shock of seeing my first cricket ball. I simply couldn't believe that there was anything so dangerous loose in what up to then had seemed a safe sort of world. A terrible master at a terrible prep school introduced us. 'This is the bat, Morley,' he said, 'and this is the ball', and flung it at me. A small red leather bomb, which for some reason failed to explode. I have lived in terror of the thing ever since. In vain I pleaded to be allowed to continue playing with a soft ball. 'I might even learn to like the game,' I told them, 'if I played with a soft ball.' Of course I lied. I had already played with a soft ball and hated it. My governesses were always urging me to join up with other children standing in front of groynes or spread out over the pebbles while Father bowled. (Never *my* Father, thank God.)

Blind in one eye, I discovered early on that I was never to stay long by the breakwater. While others made a meal of their innings, my own were brief to the point of incomprehension. A moment of top dogmanship holding the bat, a quick swing and back to Long Stop for the rest of time. Later at my Public School I used even to hasten the process by taking guard and then, before the ball could reach me, knocking down my wicket. A protest which enraged the jolly cricketing house captain, who beat me nightly in the bathroom.

Right-minded boys were supposed to like cricket.

The masters used to read out the scores of the country cricket matches after prayers. They believed in a God who liked cricket and prep schools named after His saints.

Not being of the faithful I particularly dread the Test Match season, always fearful that switching on the radio or television I shall be exposed to a cricket commentary by Mr. Arlott.

I cannot explain why I dread being told that Sun Yet San has now bowled more overs in his sweater from the gasworks end than any other fool in first-class cricket, but I do. Readers may think me mad if they wish. I am, but I am also brave. The other day, taking some of my old phobias out and examining them, I decided to go back to cricket for the day and to see what really goes on at Lords during a Test match. When I arrived nothing whatever was going on. It had been raining and although the sun now shone, the wicket was covered over with what appeared to be collapsed sight screens, and a number of mackintosh sheets of various sizes and colours were laid out to dry on the turf. Someone had obviously been shopping at the army surplus supply stores and was now keen to display the trophies. No one seemed keen to play cricket. While I watched, two men in blue took the field with the measured tread of police officers approaching an incident which they trust will have sorted itself out before they get there. 'Umpires inspecting the pitch,' one of the custodians informed me. They go in for custodians at Lords. Sports which were once the privilege of the few and are still run by the gentlemen of England, Polo, Cricket, Racing, concentrate as far as conditions still permit on the 'enclosure within the enclosure'. At Lords there are stands marked Members Only and others bearing the legend Friends of Members.

Always one to dramatise my situation, I asked how I could make a friend. 'It's no use today,' the custodian informed me, 'friend or no friend, it's another fifty pence.'

By now the Umpires had reached the centre of the ground, cautiously lifted one end of the tarpaulin and sniffed. I wondered what they were looking for, could it be wet grass? Inscrutably they returned to the Pavilion. I bet Mr. Betjeman likes the Pavilion, I bet he likes cricket. 'The Players,' announced the public address system, 'will take lunch . . . another inspection will be made at two-thirty.'

'But I've paid,' I told the custodian.

'You should read the small print.' No one having asked me to lunch, I lingered by his side while he reminisced about the time when as a boy they paid him sixpence for eight overs. 'Who paid sixpence?' I asked. 'Why, the players, of course . . . we were glad of the money in those days. Cricket is dying,' he went on, 'it's been dying ever since I can remember.' I went over and read the menu outside the restaurant. Everything was cold. I was cold. I took a taxi and went to an Indian restaurant up the road. If I wasn't going to watch them playing cricket at least I could watch them cooking my lunch.

When I got back they were ringing bells, just like they used to at St. Christopher's. An Indian stood outside the Tavern shouting at one of the players coming out to field. 'Encouraging him?' I asked. 'He is my kid brother, he insulted my mother, now he can never go back to India. I shall cut him in small pieces.' He insisted on buying me a gin and tonic. 'Keep the bottle to throw later,' he advised. He was a very cheerful fellow.

I sat down beside a man who knew all about it. He had spent a lifetime playing and watching the game, a helpless hopeless addict. Perhaps he was happy, perhaps they were all happy, even the little man in a turban who bowled and kept rearranging the fieldsmen and seemed more grown up than all the others. The Father figure on the sands, he bowled all through the long afternoon, slowly, cunningly, patiently, and the children got out one after another, trying to prolong their time at the wicket, not really scoring, just staying there so they shouldn't have to field in their turn. Nothing had changed. Halfway through the afternoon I found myself almost enjoying myself. It was the bars, I suppose. Lords is full of bars and barmaids. I always like barmaids. 'We come down from Lincoln every morning,' one of them told me. 'We enjoy the change.' If they could why couldn't I? The very last ball of the very last over bowled Edrich. He had stopped trying to score half an hour earlier. He wanted to bat another day. I was glad he went.

94

I watched them all go home, the old men and the boys, the mothers and the custodians, the waitresses from Lincoln, the decent quiet people of England – and, oh my God, you should have seen the filth they left behind.

FAR-AWAY
PLACES
WITH
STRANGE-SOUNDING
NAMES

Away From It All

I have a friend who spends a fair amount of his life on junkets. He is a travel correspondent – the cinnamon on the holiday custard. I thought it might be worth asking him where he spends his own holiday. 'Reading,' he told me. Quite a large town, in Berkshire, but I had never heard of anyone going there for a spree. He chooses it for that very reason. He does not want to be too comfortable and in Reading, apparently, there are any number of small, private hotels which are really mean – mean with the butter, mean with the bathwater, mean with just about everything. The bedrooms still have linoleum on the floor and a light which switches out by the door. No soap, either. It is such little things which count with him.

It is always fatal to ask an expert. Me, I go for the swinging holiday. I have always yearned for the sort of Mediterranean clubland where they wear bead necklaces and shorten them every time they need a drink or a partner – missionary stuff in reverse. I used to like the idea of dug-out canoes and small desert islands with tree-climbing crabs – until I made a film in Tahiti. I've tried boating in the Aegean, submerging in the Bosporus. I have dunked myself cautiously in the Pacific, paddled in the Indian Ocean. And then come happily home to Folkestone where it all started. I can still remember digging down furiously to reach Australia which some fool nurse had explained was underfoot.

In those days I wore striped cotton bathing costumes and shining white sailor suits with a genuine whistle on Sundays, when we didn't go down on the beach until after church parade. I wore the same sort of linen hat that I wear now, because I have a dream that one day some elderly crone in a Bath chair will pass me, a large and portly figure sandcastling for the grandchildren, and observe to her companion that I am the same dear little chap who used to dig there when she was a girl and I haven't changed a bit.

For most holiday wear, however, I shop nowadays at special boutiques which cater for the fuller figure and have names like 'Big and Beautiful' or 'Giant Strides' or 'High and Mighty'. I see people looking at me out of the

99

corner of their eye when I'm in a bathing suit and saying to themselves, 'So that's what happens if you let yourself go.'

Myself, I cannot understand the craze for the body beautiful and the deep tan. *I* look out of the corner of *my* eye and notice the hiatuses – the last little bit of the canvas which stays obstinately white and spoils the picture. It's not that I'm jealous, but I can't help wondering how long it has all taken. And I resent the unhooked brassière, the face in the sand, the essential inanimation of steak on a charcoal broiler. I find this basting such a bore: so much cold cream squeezed out of tubes and spread endlessly over the torso and then the awful problem of the back and sides. Where to stop? Occasionally I employ a Flit spray-gun and little bubbles of oil burst and trickle down my chest.

On a beach, I am happier to be off and into the sea. The fat float easily. And I have found that each time I come out I am obliged to start again with the suntan treatments. I lose heart, and finish up in my bathing wrap. With burnt insteps. This is not to say that I do not enjoy holidays, I thoroughly enjoy shopping for sandals and buying the funny-tummy preparations. I appreciate the feel of the air-tickets in my wallet. Indeed, I count the days to freedom as I lie around at home with my eyes shut, telling myself that in a week's time I will be doing just that on the Lido. And sure enough, when I get to the Lido, I am happy to be Away From It All.

Though not entirely, of course. My feelings are perhaps best summed up by another friend, a bookmaker, whom I once asked why he chose Venice every year. 'I like it,' said the fellow. 'I don't say it's perfect: for one thing, you can't get the greyhound track results unless you ring up home – but nowhere has everything, has it?' How true.

Mr Morley, I Presume

Of all the madness I experienced as a child, nothing reached a higher quotient of insanity than the geography lessons. I was instructed to draw the course of the Euphrates River and to mark and name the principal tributaries. Who was I at the age of eight to decide the relative eminence of rivers? I still do not know where the Euphrates rises and falls. I sometimes wonder whether, indeed, the Euphrates is still rising and falling, so seldom do I hear it mentioned. And even today, as I travel the globe, I am still trying to hide the fact that I have only the haziest idea of how the world fits together and why, for example, when flying out of Britain, I must pause at Frankfurt en route to Kenya. I had decided on Kenya for a holiday, because if one is to bask in the sun, it's smart to get as close to the equator as possible. Mombasa is not only near the equator, it is thoroughly spoiled. I am not one for the unspoiled terrain, the empty beach, the thornbush, the flyblown kiosk with the lukewarm beverage. Give me the marble terrace, the steps leading down into the water. I can ignore the high-rise apartment at my back. I am looking the other way.

When I leave the water, I like elegant patio furnishings and a cool drink – not out of the coconut but from the refrigerator. I like the loving care of the barman, not the childlike friendliness of the noble savage. I am not interested in ecology. I refuse to worry about the fate of the spotted hartebeest. If it's had its day, that's all right with me. I shall manage without the creature. On the other hand, when it's hot, I prefer not to manage without ice and air conditioning. Why should I?

It was exceedingly hot in Mombasa. I had only to put my nose outside and the skin peeled. Fellow visitors coated their features with cream and wore plastic shields. My world was full of the chicken-mayonnaise crowd and I was content to lie in the shade behind some rocks and watch a honeymooning French couple play chess every afternoon under a coconut tree.

In the bar one evening I met a man who had a house in Lamu, a town farther up the East African coast toward Italian Somaliland; and the next morning I was flying there. I decided against making the journey by road and dugout canoe through the mango swamps, as I didn't fancy having to stand upright in the latter, watched by rapacious crocodiles. When we landed, the pilot warned us against taking photographs of the ground staff, who were convicts. They seemed remarkably young to be serving prison sentences. But farther along the path to the jetty and the motorboat that was to take us across the lagoon to the town itself, we came upon a more mature group breaking stones.

In Lamu, I was welcomed by the curator of the museum, who introduced me to his parrot. The parrot came from London and hadn't learned to fly, on account of a defective wing. Each afternoon at four local time, which is petshop closing time in Britain, the parrot insisted on being put to bed in a dark room with the door locked. Until that happened, he screamed.

The rest of the town came from *Alice in Wonderland*. Once upon a time, Lamu was the richest port on the coast, with plumbing far in advance of anything Europe had experienced up to then – including the bidet. Wealthy residents even drove gold rods into the walls of the houses by way of ostentation. Little remains of the elegant extravagance that demanded four slaves to a canopy as the local sherifs paraded the main street. The sherifs still parade, holding their own umbrellas; the sons of the prophets are everlastingly marrying the daughters of the faithful, and everlastingly divorcing them the next morning. A night with a sherif for her virgin daughter, and mother goes to heaven, or so they tell her.

A great deal remains in Lamu, including even the British. There are many cannons on the waterfront and a plethora of bones in the sands beneath. Lamu played a home match around 1800 against the neighbouring island of Pate and won 1700 to 6 – a famous massacre, as when the tide went out suddenly, the away team couldn't get off the reef. Usually when Lamu lost, she lost to the cannibal tribes, the Portuguese, the Ethiopians and, of course, the British.

One afternoon I lunched on my hotel terrace and noticed the beach being patrolled by soldiers. The oldest of all the English residents had taken to exposing himself by the water's edge and the newly-appointed district commissioner was determined for some reason to catch him in the act. 'Will they shoot him?' I asked anxiously. 'They won't even catch him,' I was told. 'His wife is keeping him indoors.'

Later, I signed the visitors' book immediately below the Aga Khan, who had just left. There is one family in Lamu that subscribes to his faith and he had taken pains to meet them, but not while he was alone. If you are a follower of the Aga's and catch him alone, he must accede to your request. The family was anxious to buy the local mosque at a knockdown price, knock it down and build a hotel. The Aga Khan was courteous, circumspect and perpetually accompanied on his walks along the waterfront.

On the way back from Lamu I stopped in Malindi, Kenya, to lunch with the British and take tea with the Krauts. Nationalism is encouraged by the package tour. The Germans are winning hands down; there are at least four jumbo flights each week from Frankfurt. Of the Americans, there is little sign along the coast. They simply haven't the time to lie around in the sun; besides, that sort of life comes easier and cheaper at home. If they come to this part of Africa at all, it is to Mombasa or Nyali Beach, and then only for two or three nights, to rest up between safaris. Americans are in the game game, and how well they play it. The men try to look and dress like Stewart Granger; the women favour Dorothy Lamour — the head turbaned, the figure sheathed in fiery African colors. They are armed with cameras, not rifles; zoom lenses, not cartridges.

There is not really a great deal to buy in Africa, but Americans have a stab at shopping. Occasionally, they are stabbed themselves. One party, in particular, was nearly speared to death by the Masai because they laughed too loudly and bent themselves double, pretending to have been wounded by the dancers' spears. The tribesmen, suddenly bored by audience participation, decided to play it for real. None of the visitors was killed, but the guilty tribe was punished by being deprived of the dance concession for a spell.

Some tourists also ask for trouble by stepping out of jeeps to feed an elephant the remains of a picnic lunch or by climbing down from a tree hut to proffer a leopard a drink. Punishment when it comes is condign; an elephant takes its time trampling a man to death. When it's finished, all that's left is a thin, red mush.

Of course, not all trouble is invited. There can be no harm, surely, in tea on the lawn and no blame atached to anyone, except the lioness herself, if she chooses to hunt and catch a baboon among the chocolate biscuits and buttered scones. 'Two of my guests finished up in trees and quite an old lady up to her neck in the pond,' Mr. Pascoe told me. Mr. Pascoe is manager of the appropriately named Hunter's Lodge, which stands just to the side of the Nairobi — Mombasa highway. 'We have a good many lions here,' he went on proudly. 'I usually take guests for an evening ramble and we nearly always see something, even if it's only a snake.'

Water-holes are a great feature of the game lodges. Floodlit and with a thoughtfully-provided artificial salt lick, they provide an opportunity for the game to have a look at the guests in their natural habitat. All day the latter have been bouncing around in jeeps, making it difficult for the elephant and particularly the leopard to count them accurately. But here, bunched at the bar, they can be inspected by the wart hogs and hyenas at leisure.

Sitting next to me at the bar was a Kenya policeman's wife, who had lived in Africa all her life and who knew a good deal about the Mau Mau. 'We had a cook in those days,' she told me, 'who was one in a thousand, the kindest, most obliging, most dedicated cook in all of Africa, famous for his spaghetti soufflé. With this talented man in the kitchen, I couldn't go wrong as a hostess and he might have stayed forever, had not my husband come home one evening and told me that our splendid chef was the senior Mau Mau oath administrator for miles around. It was a terrible oath, you know,' she continued, 'the worst sort of black magic and quite unmentionably obscene. Arrangements were made that he be arrested in his own village because he was such a charming old man. That night the fellow cooked his last soufflé, or so we thought, and the next day we drove him back to his home, where a dozen soldiers were waiting. He got into the truck and bumped off to prison and, as we thought again, his death. Then about three months later, my husband and I went to dinner at the home of the police commissioner. The meal began with spaghetti soufflé.'

I asked her about problems confronting white Kenyans these days and she thought cattle rustling was as serious as any. The whole farming economy is undermined by the necessity of enclosing the stock every evening. It means cows can't be left out to pasture but have to be driven into pounds. Their grazing is interrupted and the milk yield and growth rate are far lower than they should be. When cattle are stolen, the farmer must do everything possible to recover his beasts, otherwise he will lose more of them next time. The thieves have to be tracked, sometimes for weeks, and all other work on the farm comes to a standstill; and when the cattle are found they have to be driven home and they lose more weight in the process.

My companion was one of the few white Kenyans I met who didn't seem affronted by the way things were going. The others always prefaced their opinions by confiding how long they had lived in Kenya. They felt a peculiar sense of injustice at the nationalism they were now encountering. Whatever their attitude had been before independence, they no longer clapped their hands and shouted for Charley. When they spoke to their African servants, they almost whispered their requests, couching them in the reasonable terms in which one might address a difficult seven-year-old. 'Don't scream,' they seemed to be pleading, 'and don't stamp your foot, but just run along like a good boy and see if you can find Mummy a little more ice. Won't that be fun, now?'

How much fun the Africans have these days is difficult to assess. The women lead lives of incredible austerity; each day they must walk miles in search of firewood and to fetch water from the communal tap. They also must do the housework and till the fields and mind the herds and contrive at the same time to dress elegantly and to carry their youngest on their back.

For men, life is easier. Unless, that is, they elect to work in the hotels, where they must watch the guests waste the bath water and leave the food untouched on their plates. What do they think of the luxury in which we wallow, compared with the deprivation and undernourishment of their own folk? I asked the proprietor of Leisure Lodge, arguably the most comfortable and certainly the most beautiful hotel in Kenya. He told me that the African wasn't undernourished, that most Europeans were far from clean and only with the greatest reluctance would he be willing to entertain one in his home. This was particularly true of hippies, whose physical presence nauseated him.

According to the proprietor, his staff had no need to work; they were all possessed of small-holdings that brought them adequate incomes. They worked in order to pay for more wives. The acquisition of wives was a complicated and lengthy game. 'It is played,' he explained, 'rather like Monopoly.'

'But if you were an African awakened in the night by your child crying for a drink of water, how would you feel if you knew the nearest tap was five miles away?' I asked. 'Would you go yourself? Would you send your wife?'

'I would wake my wife,' he told me, 'and she would give the child a coconut or a glass of goat's milk. Very few Africans drink water.'

I wasn't sure whether I believed him or not. I recalled the experience of one settler who had taken his head cattleman, a Masai tribesman, to the Royal Show in London last summer. After two days he was asked what had struck him most forcibly. 'Those taps,' he said, 'all those taps.'

There is a man called Donovan Maule, an actor like myself, who went to Nairobi after the last war and decided to stay and found a stock company. Curiously enough, he made a fortune, retired and built himself and his wife a bungalow on a creek near Mombasa. The theatre is now run by his daughter. They still play Rattigan and Coward and Priestley and

Maugham, but the heart and the profit have gone out of the business. 'A lot of our patrons have had to pack up and go home. They don't like it, you know; England isn't what it was, any more than this place. What they dread most is having to retire to somewhere like Canterbury.' He poured me another gin and slapped his wrist. 'We don't get mosquitoes here, you known.'

'Nor in Canterbury,' I told him, but he seemed unconvinced.

In what was once called the White Highlands, beyond the Aberdare mountain range, the British still farm the land, but no longer with the confidence they used to display when the Mau Mau was around and each settler had a gun at the ready. They have put their guns away but still greet the stranger on their stoop with caution. They know that his briefcase hides no fearsome machete, but more probably just a letter from the President himself, inquiring in the politest possible manner whether perhaps the present owner might care to sell his property. After that, of course, it's only a matter of time before Canterbury, or a bungalow near Mombasa, becomes a reality.

The mission pilot was on his honeymoon and lived in Abyssinia. He was the only man I saw in Africa actually eat a coconut and he did it with expert ease, even producing a bowl for the milk. He had been married only three days, which was perhaps why, in true African fashion, he neglected to offer his wife any until he had almost finished it. There was plenty of coconut meat for both of them, and as he munched, he explained why he found it necessary to spend an hour on his knees each week, specifically asking the Almighty to put an end to the permissive society in West London.

'Are you praying for a holocaust?' I asked him.

'If necessary.'

'Tell me,' I urged, 'about Addis Ababa. Is it true the penalty for stealing is to cut off a hand?'

'Sometimes.'

'My goodness,' I told him, 'I wouldn't like to see that sort of thing in Britain. Think of the number of one-armed shoppers you'd meet. I think I prefer the permissive society.'

On my last night in Africa, I hired a launch in order to inspect the carmine bee-eaters. Extraordinary birds, which look like psychedelic starlings, who choose to roost each evening in one particular clump of mango trees three or four miles upstream from the creek on which stands the Mnarani Country Club. The club is an elegant establishment, much patronized by big-game fishermen and, especially, the present Lady

Delamere. The murder case in which her husband, Delves Broughton, was tried and acquitted of the killing of 'Boy' Errol in the Fifties still provokes raised eyebrows and lowered voices wherever two or three Kenyans are gathered together with a stranger who will listen to the tale.

Upstream, we dawdled by the riverbank. I was convinced the boatman was uncertain which mango clump harboured the birds. But no, it was too early and they hadn't yet arrived. Meanwhile, he showed me huge pelicans perched in banyan trees and egrets fishing from the bank and sea eagles circling above and, rounding a bend of the river, a village built on the mud flats with children calling us to come closer and be inspected for cigarettes. My boatman ignored them and, turning the boat suddenly, brought us back downstream. He's lost, I told myself, we'll not find them now, it will be too dark to see. Then suddenly the carmine bee-eaters came swooping and soaring, settling for a moment and then flying away, and returning, and all the time the beat of their wings and the sound of their voices filled the air with excitement.

This is Africa, I told myself. This is what I came to see, and wondered if it was true that these were the only carmine bee-eaters in the world and this the only mango swamp they patronized. But when it was quiet again and darkness fell and we journeyed back downstream to the country club, I found myself considering for the hundredth time the riddle of Delves Broughton.

The rip-roaring days are over for the British. Now they walk abroad as delicately as the Japanese. In Kenya, they are remembered, but without gratitude. They set an example of incorruptibility in the administration that has not been followed. They planted sisal and grew groundnuts and became croppers. They left Kenya no richer than they found it, but look, an African will tell you, look what they got out of it for themselves.

The Desert Shall Rejoice . . .

Exactly halfway between Ouarzazate and Taroudant the car developed a nervous cough. Dusk is the hour of apprehension for the tourist, and my wife voiced the general dismay.

'I don't think I'd care for a night in the desert with this car; its engine is air-cooled.'

'I don't see what that's got to do with it,' I told her.

'If you're dying of thirst,' she reminded me, 'drink the water from the radiator first.'

Considering my spouse cleans her teeth with Evian when abroad, I couldn't really picture her under a hood letting antifreeze drip between parched lips.

'At least,' I pointed out, 'when darkness falls we will only have ourselves to worry about; most of the inhabitants have the responsibility of their flocks.'

Although there was no sign of one at the moment, we had earlier in the day passed herds of sheep and goats and an occasional camel grazing just off the tarmac or perched in a thorn tree. I didn't spot a sheep or a camel aloft, but the goats crouched like cats in the branches, munching the prickles with evident enjoyment.

Apart from them there didn't seem a lot going on in southern Morocco; the goatherders would wave and flourish iguanas indicating their desire to trade, but we had already spent our dirhams on rock quartz purchased at the roadside stalls. It was difficult to imagine what we were going to do with such quantities of crude cobalt and amethyst. There are, after all, only a limited number of doors to be stopped and papers to be weighted down back home.

I fell to wondering, while waiting for the car's expiring paroxysm, why, since sheep and goats get on so well together, such emphasis is laid on their final separation by the Bible and our own Samuel Beckett. 'My brother looks after the goats and I look after the sheep' – or was it the other way round? I never quite understood what *Waiting for Godot* was about, but here surely, on this desolate plain, was the right setting for those sad tramps.

Then, too, I recalled how once, preparing to be honoured by the Monarch, I had ascended the red-carpeted staircase at Buckingham Palace to have a ribbon hung round my proud neck, and at the top found two separate queues of grateful subjects and a court gentleman interrogating us for all the world as if we were back at our first party playing Oranges and Lemons.

'Are you,' he asked each of us in turn, 'a sheep or a goat?' The goats (CBE's, naturally) preceded the sheep (OBE's). Here in the Dras Valley, where the guidebook claimed the Saadins once captured the kingdom of Marrakesh from the hands of the Merinides, I don't think I'd mind much which I was, just, thank Allah, as long as I wasn't born a donkey.

The car seemed to have escaped pneumonia but still appeared to be suffering from chronic bronchitis, and we stopped at a garage to explain its symptoms and get another opinion. The attendant diagnosed a shortage of gasoline and lack of air in the tyres. I paid and left, clutching my guidebook tightly. It must be difficult to write a guidebook on Morocco, so thinly is excitement spread on the ground.

In Italy, by contrast, there is always something to observe. The most insignificant village has a church with murals, at least, attributed to a pupil of Tiepolo, or a curious relic in the sacristy of San Piero a Grado. In France there are restaurants worth a detour, ruined châteaux, abandoned viaducts. Even in Britain there is usually something of exquisite boredom to be avoided with gratitude. 'From the village a rough track leads after a mile to a small Roman burial mound', or 'On the south side of the town and on the banks of the river is Bantam Manor, once the ancestral home of the Somerset family and now closed (as always) to the public'.

Mr Fodor, in *Morocco 1975,* although never completely at a loss, is often hard put to it and tries just about everything from 'How to become a Hadj' and 'Courtly love and Aristotle', to the information that 'close to the Ourika the Almoravides set up their first headquarters at . . .' Go to the top of the class, Ahmed.

For the tourist, luckily, there is no class and no exam – unless he is still at school and expected when he gets home to write a paper on the founding of the Saadin dynasty. For most of us, guidebook information doesn't so much go in one ear and out the other as never go in one ear at all. Even when reading aloud to a companion about, for instance, the ancestral home of El Glaoui, I seldom seemed to be listening.

109

I was pleasurably surprised, therefore, to find how much I was looking forward to visiting the palm groves of Skoura. I seemed for once to be sharing Mr Fodor's enthusiasm for the treat ahead. 'In these parts,' so the author assured me, 'roses grow as thick as crabgrass on a suburban lawn, enough of them to provide the whole country with much appreciated rose water.' Skoura apparently looks 'like a fairyland when the roses bloom, and the green palm trees form a background for a group of pretty kasbahs.'

In order to reach the promised land, however, we had to drive from the Gazelle D'Or – a fairly expensive hotel at Taroudant where I was currently toasting my pale winter hide to a fiery red – some five hundred miles across the wastelands of southern Morocco. We spent one night en route at the oasis of Ouarzazate. The Hotel du Sud is much frequented by package pilgrims but offers accommodations of exquisite discomfort. We were offered a bedroom, the door of which sported a hole where the handle had been removed, and with lighting so meagre that only in the loo could one see to read.

The Maroc Tourist Motel is quite a cut above it, and it would have been perfectly possible to sleep there except for guard dogs scenting perpetual intruders, or just possibly merely baying at the moon. Although, strictly speaking, the desert doesn't officially start at Ouarzazate, everything else more or less stops there, so we were delighted to find, about ten miles outside the town on the way to Skoura, a signpost pointing to a dam and a glimpse of blue water in the distance.

We decided to have a tilt at the sand dunes, and the little car was never quite the same again. The ruined village on the edge of the reservoir was destined one day to be covered with water but completion was apparently some way off and the waters seemed to be actually receding. We hunted for turtles, and I was badly scared by a shepherd dog. Rabies is one thing I can do without, as I explained to my companions whilst unlocking the car doors from the inside to let them in later. Apparently the brute was tamer than I had imagined and had accepted the last of the chocolate with every appearance of cordiality, as indeed I would have myself had I been offered it.

The roses of Skoura were palpably not in bloom, and the whole place was very far from what I was expecting. We parked the car in the shade and tried a gateway from which tourists were emerging with inscrutable expressions and cameras still in their holsters. A young man volunteered to guide us through the Garden of the Military, to reach which we had to pass the ritual rubbish heap. The Moroccans excel in arranging refuse –

Coca-Cola bottles, dusty cardboard and tin cans – to simulate Japanese rock gardens, and are careful to site it where visitors are best able to admire their efforts at local preservation. The military gardens were dusty, overgrown, unwatered, unweeded, uncared for and altogether hopeless.

'Where are the roses?' I asked, and then suddenly came upon a small bush with a solitary bud encrusted with brown fly. 'They will open in May,' the guide assured us. 'In May the roses are very fine.'

We thanked him and turned the car around and headed back for Taroudant, and now that we were nearly there the car appeared to be breathing a shade more easily and so was I. The Moroccans squatting by the roadside or trudging along it, tented against the dust and the evening chill, waved a greeting and we waved back. Waving or drowning? I found it difficult to decide. What sort of life is it for a small goatherd or a large Arab lady plodding behind a donkey laden with firewood? I wish I could share Mr Fodor's belief that in a land not exactly overflowing with milk and honey, a Moroccan prefers to keep his own goats and bees rather than shop in the supermarket – that he wants no part of the twentieth-century rat race. The car managed to get us back in time for baths and dinner and the news that the swimming pool was successfully filling up once more.

Tomorrow we shall sit beside it and boast of our adventure and realize that soon we must leave the hot sun and the shady souk and fly home to British weather and the economic crisis, soaring inflation and plunging stock market reports. I shan't be altogether sorry to miss the roses at Skoura; I suppose I am not really the orange blossom type. Give me good old carbon monoxide any day – well, most days.

Six Days on the Waterfront

(A Hong Kong Diary)

Saturday. Arrived – as is often the case in these parts – in time for the Saturday races. General Penfold, who commands the track, took us in hand. 'It's not so easy for him as it was in the army,' his wife explained. 'He has to see to everything himself. In the forces they take care of the details.' I saw what she meant when the General detached himself from the party on our way to the elevators to restrain a china-clearing fatigue intent on sharing our transport.

We were en route to the Jardine Mathieson box to pay a courtesy call; everyone is polite to Jardine Mathieson in Hong Kong. There is an atmosphere of old Vienna about the race boxes. Friends, possibly lovers, drop in and there is talk of other things besides the performance. Taipans mingle. We found Eartha Kitt struggling to persuade her hosts to sponsor her on the morrow on her walk round the island. 'I want everyone to give me ten dollars a mile,' she announced. 'Do you know what it costs to run a hospital out here?' There was not much audible speculation. 'I really must get my husband to help,' one lady told her. 'Where has he got to? Ah yes, there he is, talking to Mr. Wang. One mustn't interrupt.'

The horses raced round and round on a small sandy track; when not circulating they live in flats on the premises. 'Elevators?' I enquired, but was told they were expected to walk up. More money goes through the Tote on one afternoon than they take the whole of Ascot week. Soon the new racecourse will open. They plan to have races twice a week in the future and no wonder.

'We get quite a lot of your profession coming through here,' the General told me. 'Tomlinson, Dave Allen and now this fellow Hadleigh is here.' 'Harper,' his wife corrected him, 'he's called Gerald Harper.' 'My wife's pin-up,' the General confided. 'I'm not absolutely certain about the fellow myself, almost too good to be true.' Homing back to the Mandarin from the Happy Valley, a distance as the crow flies of about a mile, we have travelled five. One proceeds in orbit, encapsulated on the freeway, searching for a re-entry corridor.

Sunday. 'Would you like,' said Peter Stafford, who made the Mandarin one of the best hotels in the world, 'a tour of the new territories?' I am not an expansionist by instinct but the phrase had good buoyant colonial ring. 'I'll lay on a car and a picnic.' We travelled in a Rolls-Royce — I kept hoping everyone would think I was the Governor. The new territories are dotted with new towns. Here, as on the island, building is compulsive — enormous blocks of flats, some still encased with delicate bamboo scaffolding. Not quite the same frenetic leapfrogging as on Hong Kong Island, where one day they build a new skyscraper hotel and the next a water tower to block out the view. Forty storeys high you're still practically in the basement.

We picnic in a temple — well, just outside, watch the faithful or possibly just the superstitious approach the altars and shake the box. Out falls a numbered wand, one of many, and then the priest looks up the number in the book and tells them what they've won; an English tourist joins in and is told she can look forward to a bleak period for some time but through it wisdom will come. Not to play the numbers possibly.

On the way home we stop to watch a Chinese Opera, no charge for admittance, performed in a huge and beautiful temporary structure of bamboo and silver paper.

Monday. Our day for Macao; you can go by Hovercraft or Super Hovercraft, skimming the China Sea past the islands and the junks and arriving after just over an hour to stand for another three-quarters while they examine the visas and bumf, filled out wrongly as usual in my case. How I would love once in my life to get all the right answers on all the right lines. Also to remember my passport number.

Don't quite know what to see first but decide to go to the shipping office and book our return tickets on the regular ferry. The Hovercraft stops at dusk and we plan to visit the casino in the evening. Shipping office quite difficult to find, no one seems to want to speak pidgin English, and all the inhabitants seem depressed. We find the shipping office and I decide to splurge on a V.I.P. cabin on the midnight boat. It sounds so grand and anyway casinos bring out a latent extravagance in me. We walk past the junks moored along the waterfront and inhale the fish drying in the sun. Some rather fine colonial buildings. Portugal came and, I suppose, went.

We have a poor luncheon and a drive in an ex-London doubledecker over the causeway to nowhere in particular. We come back and I decide to break the bank. No one else seems even to be trying. One can only play roulette on one's own for a limited time. By six-thirty I am ready to call it a day; we catch an earlier steamer. No V.I.P. cabins left but we are very comfortable in the television lounge and have a rather bad dinner but tonic water is again available on board, which it wasn't on Macao. One is really cut off without tonic water. I miss it more than the glossies.

Tuesday. Do the Island. Up in the cable car to the peak, down by taxi to Aberdeeen. Short half-hour dash round the harbour in sampan punted by buxom Chinese housewife. Every time I see a dog I wonder if it's tomorrow's lunch. Fellow tourists told us they were offered some in the new territory and that it smelt really delicious. Oh well, there are worse places to live than on a Chinese houseboat. No compulsory education and quite a lot of money to be made when grandmother decides to go fishing. I keep wondering about the loo.

We avoid the Chinese floating restaurants and lunch at the Old Vic, a smart new eatery run by the Hilton with photographs of Lewis Waller and Irene Vanbrugh on the walls and good pub fare – rather better in fact.

There is quite a spate of Olde Worlde pubs, built by Hutchinsons, but now under new management. Some of the names around here are said quietly, others spoken with confidence. No one says 'Slater Walker' out loud.

In the evening give a dinner party at Gaddis for the General and keep Gerald Harper up my sleeve till he appears, his elegant self fresh from filming at the Star Ferry. The General likes him enormously, a real coup de télévision. Tremendously impressed by my new neighbour who is here for the Mandarin Sotheby sale (not the hotel, just jade and jewellery). He has come to sell, not to buy and not in the sale. 'Tell me about jade,' I ask, and he obligingly takes the stuff from waxed paper packets which he carries around in his waistcoat pockets because of insurance.

'The price?' I murmur. He shrugs. 'Say sixty thousand pounds this small one.' When he has gone I pick up his coffee cup. I had the strangest feeling he had left something under it.

Wednesday. Go on a junket to the other islands. No one but ourselves and two Australians in the party. Ask why the trip isn't more popular with fellow tourists and am told no one has seven hours to spare in Hong Kong. The islands are beautiful, peaceful, perfect. We lunch at 'Ned Kelly's Last Stand', a beach restaurant, and I have clams. How daring one gets. On the way back through the village in a small darkened corner of a house sits an

Old Chinese lady assembling plastic motor cars – putting on the wheels. My wife watches with fascination. 'Oh, the hours,' she tells me, 'I've spent doing just that.'

Back in the Mandarin for the Sotheby sale on closed circuit TV. Hotel guests can bid by telephone but somehow we never get round to it. Disappointed that only the gems are shown, not the bidders. Most of the stuff goes mysteriously to a Mrs. Moore in Washington. Can she be linked by satellite? There seems no end to jade. I realise I don't even know where it comes from. Are there jade mines or jade alluvial deposits or is it washed ashore like ambergris? Mrs. Penfold owns two small jade drops which she wears occasionally at cocktail parties. The Chinese ladies always come over and admire them, entirely disregarding the necklace from which they hang.

There is a star ruby which I would like to bid for but before I can lift the phone it's knocked down, to Mrs. Moore naturally, for a hundred thousand pounds or thereabouts. I don't suppose I should have bought it anyway. Just telly shopping. I feel for the first time in Hong Kong that I am saving money.

Decide to dine at restaurant called Cock and Pheasant. Wife urges me to book but caution restrains. When we arrive it is absolutely and entirely empty. 'Looking for friendees,' I tell them. 'Have to meetee. Come again quick time.' They don't believe me, I don't believe myself, in any case it's an English restaurant, I think, but why is it empty? We go to another huge hotel, this one isn't only empty, it's freezing. The air-conditioning has gone mad. Along a corridor private dining-rooms invite, but not us, alas. Mr Fang's private party. Mr Lee's ditto. Doctor Fu Manchu's? The tables are laid with snowy tablecloths and tea cups. But the guests haven't shown up yet though it's past nine. In the public eating-room there are also empty tables, and a view of the harbour, but the cold persists. We beat another retreat and finish up at the Old Vic. Back at the hotel the television is still switched on but now shows *The Hireling*. It is on view all through the night. 'Who,' I ask Peter Stafford, 'watches films at three in the morning?' 'Jet laggers,' he tells me.

Thursday. Our last day. Shopping, shopping, shopping. I buy a Mickey Mouse electronic calculator and work out how many hours I've lived. Quite a surprise. Hope the grandson will like it but if not shall be happy to take it back. Chinese goods on sale at the Chinese Communist Shop. Bargaining not encouraged, but beautiful useless jade trees hung with semi-precious stones. Beautiful, useless paintings, and for my son something useful at last, a stage set of an opera under a glass cloche. Promise faithfully to carry it. Buy sandalwood fans, Chinese wall paintings, kimonos, embroidered shirts, jade fruits, the sort of things you can't get in England. Unless, of course, you happen to be in Harrod's where I was this week and saw the whole caboodle at prices marginally cheaper than we paid.

The plane was delayed due to political go-slows in Australia. In the V.I.P. lounge we met up with Tarquin Olivier and some of his directors. He works for De La Rue. 'Ah yes,' I told them graciously, 'far and away the best playing cards.' 'Bank notes,' he corrected me gently. 'We sell banknotes.' 'Those, too,' I assured him.

That's what Hong Kong is all about, I suppose. The last place in the world where money is still in fashion.

I was so glad to have seen it while it was still there. A Lewis Carroll conception where you keep running twice as fast to stay in the same place. Can the young men fresh from British counting-houses still make a fortune out here? What happens when the lease is up? The stallholders up and down the ladder streets selling sea kale by the root and deers' antlers, live chickens and dead snakes, century-old eggs covered in clay and very small, live catfish in plastic bags to flavour the rice bowls.

Why is everyone so insanely cheerful? Is there no such thing as a *plain* Chinese child? Back on the jumbo and heigh-ho for the simple life. Would you care to try the Sydney Rock Oysters or the caviare? We shall be in Teheran just after dawn but for security reasons transit passengers will not be permitted to leave the plane. I am sure you will enjoy our film, it's about an English vet.

On Taipeh Island the day before yesterday I was watching them building a junk. They cost about as much as a bungalow in Thames Ditton. Now's my chance, I told myself and enquired about the loo. The guide shook his head. 'But how do they manage?' I persisted. 'Round the corner,' he told me. 'Round the corner, in the middle of the ocean.' Damn clever, these Chinese.

On Location with The Blue Bird

When, some six or seven years ago, I first visited Leningrad, it was in the company of one destined by fate to become the theatre critic of *Punch*. We were struck by the frequency with which roast partridge featured on the menus of the various hotels and restaurants where we ate. We were, of course, impressed by the treasure trove of the Hermitage and by the beauty of the palaces which bordered the Neva as well, but what intrigued us almost as much as Tsarkoye Selo was our never-ending quest for the dish which we never succeeded in tasting.

How strange, therefore, that I should now return to play a part in the film of *The Blue Bird*, an almost equally elusive creature, and find both it and the roast partridge featured but still missing.

The search for *The Blue Bird* is naturally a good deal more organised than my own haphazard scouting around the city once work is ended for the day. The formidable expedition party, led by George Cukor, includes Elizabeth Taylor, Ava Gardner, Jane Fonda, Cicely Tyson and experienced British trappers such as Richard Pearson and George Cole. As keen readers of gossip columns will have gathered, the expedition has encountered some set-backs and one or two of the original party have returned to base; but we now seem in reasonably good shape and are currently exploring The Kingdom of the Future.

Meanwhile, I have been exploring the possibility of having a really good meal in the city without speaking one word of the language. The most delicious dish I came across quite by chance in the Khirov Central Park of Culture and Rest on the Island of Yelagin along the Livogo canal. Sitting in the sun I consumed three blinis, or, as we might say, doughnuts filled with savoury mince, and debated for some time whether to carry another half-dozen back for supper, but decided they were at their best eaten warm and washed down with the local beer.

The Leningrad hotel, which is the newest and best-equipped for the tourist trade, houses a number of restaurants and cafés, of which by far the best is the Russian Tea Shop on the fourth floor. The tea and the caviare are very fine, and the ladies who preside and bear an uncanny resemblance to the Gabor sisters proffer delicious pastries and homemade plum jam.

It is better to eat at one of the small bistro-type bars in the hotel if one is in a hurry because the Russians never seem to be and believe the customer should, once he is seated, be left to ruminate on the treats in store for anything up to forty-five minutes. If, however, you are on a package tour, set meals are served you at express speeds before you are up and off again for Pushkin or the Khirov Ballet.

The Europeskiaya Hotel in Brodsky Street and the Sadko Restaurant next door are both excellent, particularly the former once you get to know the rather intimidating staff. We had Borsch and Sturgeon Moscow Style and they were both delicious. Ice cream is good all over Leningrad but here it was enlightened with plums and a liqueur.

The Volkof, in the same street as the headquarters of the K.G.B., reminds one of a gipsy tea shop of one's youth with polished tables and shawls pinned to the walls. It is entirely staffed by women and, as so often happens, we set out to have one meal and found ourselves eating another. We chose, or thought we had chosen, omelettes, river fish and pancakes, and ate sardine salad, chicken soup, roast mutton and the inevitable ice cream. Our waitress was full of apologies when she brought the bill. 'I know you ordered coffee,' she told us, 'but we're right out.'

Most patrons in restaurants seem to eat the same dishes as their neighbours on any particular evening. The menus are à la carte but the food is table d'hôte. Once you have grasped this simple fact you will stop being frustrated, and the Russians enormously enjoy the ten minutes or so spent by the visitor ordering their dream meal.

On the Nevsky Prospect the restaurants are large and crowded but the Neva and Baltiskave are worth a visit but not a queue. Eating in these places and perhaps growing impatient with the service and quality of the food, one does well to remember that the elderly party at the next table probably survived the siege and now wonders somewhat at the manners of the time.

Outside Repine, a seaside resort about fifty kilometres from the city, there is a good restaurant called The Volna where again, owing to the language barrier, I consumed cold roast beef followed, after the soup, by hot roast beef.

Russia is no gourmet's paradise any more than it is a shopping centre. There are a good many vexations to be endured by the traveller. More

118

often than not the Russian bureaucrat finds it easier, and I suspect more pleasurable, to say 'No' to the perfectly reasonable demands made upon him. Just now the accommodation of the city is stretched to the utmost and one must remember there are no empty flats, let alone office blocks, accumulating real-estate value.

This hotel caters for nearly two thousand visitors a night who in a short stay try, like myself, to form a judgement on what is happening here and how the experiment is working out after sixty or so years interrupted by war and famine.

The answer, I suppose, is that it is and it isn't. It worked out better, for instance, for Mr. and Mrs. Frank of Portland, Oregon who came here after American doctors had abandoned hope that their almost completely paralysed child could ever regain the use of his limbs. Russian surgeons operated and he's up, if not yet quite about, and due to go home in a month or two, almost fully recovered.

It didn't work so well for the mother of one of the cast who lost her luggage on the flight and was fined a rouble and a half for crossing the street with her son and jeopardising a motor car when on the way to replenish his wardrobe.

Tonight I am off to dine on S.S. Kronvert, moored near the island fort of Peter and Paul, a floating restaurant with the highest reputation. I shall order the speciality of the house, mushrooms cooked in Georgian wine, salmon with cucumber and, just for devilment, a roast partridge. I shall almost certainly eat a mixed green salad with herrings, boiled chicken and rice, and ice cream and jam. No matter. I am looking forward to it.

Raffles and the Raj

At my weight of life I avoid the pony trap. Like the Duke of Edinburgh, I need more horse power than one of those delicate creatures can provide on its own. Indeed, the last time I rode in a carrozza they stopped to bleed the horse, and with the swing to conservation gaining momentum, next time I fear they might bleed me. It took courage to climb aboard the pedal rickshaw in Singapore and I found myself apologising for my bulk in dumb show and pidgin English.

'Me much fatty? Velly solly.' But the cyclist seemed undaunted. I prayed there weren't going to be hills.

Singapore is flat on the ground and very high on the skyline. High lise is all the fashion (stop it, Molley!). We ventured into the Chinese Three-Quarters and attended a wedding. Singapore is getting rid of its slums and re-housing its poor. It has already re-housed its tourists. Where once Raffles stood alone, there are now a dozen huge American resort hotels with gourmet restaurants, swimming pools, putting greens.

Not much sign left of the British Raj but then, as I reminded myself, we did lose the place in the war. 'But steady,' I reminded myself again, 'surely we won it back?' Some very elegant Chinese in the Shangri La Hotel (where else?) tried to console me. 'We all work,' they assured me, 'for Price Waterhouse; almost all the money goes back to London.' I wish I believed them.

The food at The Hilton and the Shangri La is excellent and I can recommend the Stew Pot at the Four Seasons down by the pier, where the junks leave for the harbour tour and cargo vessels for practically everywhere else. They tell you that Singapore is the second largest harbour in the world and whisk you over the funnels in a brand new cable-car to an island half a mile out to sea.

I steadied my steed at Raffles and was disappointed in the gin sling, which was pink and weak. Raffles is where everyone tells everyone else they should stay; like the Oriental in Bangkok, it has atmosphere, rattan chairs and the ghost of Somerset Maugham. Things are a good deal livelier at the Car Park where I finished my jaunt with all feeling of guilt removed when the rickshaw rider demanded just the ten pounds for the outing. I gave him two and he professed himself delighted.

The Car Park is the great open air restaurant, a local equivalent of the Farmer's Market in Los Angeles. At six o'clock the motors leave or are flung off the lot and about three hundred stall-keepers set up shop and serve exactly what you would imagine. Cuttle fish, jumbo prawns, sweet and sour lobster, roast duck, sea urchins, dried shark, wet shark, razor fish. Everything garnished with rice cooked in a dozen different ways with a hundred different spices. I don't say every dish is a success but it's not for want of experimenting. I was reminded at times of the sort of refreshment the grandchildren prepare and urge you to try in the sand pit. I didn't come to any harm. I didn't come to any harm in Melbourne either, where the Glo Glo, the Two Faces, the Tolaro Brasserie and the Captain's Den in the Southern Cross seemed as good as ever, but I came unstuck at the Grand Metro Hotel in Vegas. Although they grudgingly accommodated me when I arrived, there was hardly a minute after my first night when the telephone wasn't ringing and an assistant manager wasn't urging me to vacate my room as it was already booked. Whenever I broached the matter at the reception desk I was assured I could stay as long as I wished, but it made no difference — back in the bedroom the phone continued to demand I quit.

On the fourth morning I asked what would happen if I decided to remain another three nights. 'You'll see what will happen, Mr. Morley,' the voice answered. There was no mistaking the threat. Vegas is a rough town: I chickened out. I can't pretend I was happy in the Grand. For one thing, the sliding doors leading to the sunken circular bath had become unhinged and gave every indication of sliding onto my head whenever I approached. All attempts to get them fixed failed, as did my request that someone come and clean the windows. I learnt later from the housekeeper that no one likes cleaning windows at the Grand as the building is too tall, and pending a contract from the East no one will put as much as a chamois leather on them even from the inside.

From my bedroom to the elevator must have been a distance of three hundred yards along corridors constantly patrolled by armed guards. When the lobby was reached there was another three hundred yards across the casino lobby to the front door. Long lines waited all day outside the coffee shop and only around the roulette wheel did comparative order and peace reign. I breakfasted daily on twenty-nine and the neighbours

121

and a complimentary cup of coffee brought to me at the table. If it was all that uncomfortable, you might ask, why stay? You will hardly believe it when I tell you that twenty-nine or thereabouts kept coming up.

I dined one night in the restaurant. The food wasn't all that special but the side dishes included a vanishing tiger, a performing elephant, a troupe of Pekingese puppies, a camel, a llama and a cheetah. We were shown clips of the late Judy Garland, and living fellow-buskers recreated the ambiance but not, alas, quite the talent of Metro-Goldwyn-Mayer's more spectacular triumphs. There was the celebrated staircase and the Busby Berkeley routines and people pretending that they were Astaire and Rogers and Fields and Cantor and Macdonald and Eddy. The celebrated Lion appeared briefly, heavily shackled and not enjoying it much either. But I think we were both impressed by the elevators. I have never seen so many. Everyone and everything arrived vertically, even the dolphin who disrobed the swimming nymphs. 'This act,' I told my companions as we chewed on the steak, 'originated in Britain, was thought up by our Mr. Paul Raymond.' We British should still take credit where possible. Indeed, we do.

Down Under

Our driver came to an abrupt halt, surveyed the long line of stationary cars ahead, and turned into a side street. He wove his way through the little township of Cooma, only to be halted once again by the same procession.

'An accident?' I asked. 'A diversion?'

'A funeral,' he told me.

In Australia headlights are switched on for the dead. The dress is formal, the women and children in deep mourning. The whole town seemed to have turned out. The mayor, perhaps, a prince of the church, a grazier of renown? At the headquarters of the Snowy Mountain Authority we gave back the key which unlocked a gate guarding a private road through the mountain, and were told it was a Mrs. Bluett who had died, the wife of a local pilot, a young woman.

We had left Canberra till last; another week and I would be on my way. In the autumn sunshine we had explored the Snowy. The river below the Jindayne Dam is now a trickle. The little town dredged from the bottom of the lake and rebuilt on the bank. New motels and petrol stations, and roads bearing the warning 'Flooded' which disappear into the water. Are there, perhaps, elderly residents who venture back at night when the tourists are safely abed, to visit their old homes, to frequent a submarine bowling green or lay a watery wreath on a tombstone?

With the coming of nuclear power stations the whole tremendous enterprise lost face. Like the Apollo Space Missions, it's the spin-offs that count: Koscusto National Park, Thredbo Alpine Village, Smiggins Holes (smorgasbord lunch at Royal Coachman), the roads for the cars, the lakes for the fishing. It's the spin-offs too, of course, which have made this tour of mine so enjoyable ever since my daughter and I touched down at Sydney Airport far too early in the morning, with the bored photographers and television interviewers camped in the press lounge day after day, asking the ritual questions of the tired traveller, needling him into an admission he had never heard of Hobart, trying to get a new quote about the dreaded Opera House, the bane of travellers. The ground staff plugging their ears and the visitors what they have come to sell. 'We open in Melbourne, it's a beaut play, come and see it when we get there, you'll have a good laugh.' A single telegram from a single relative. 'Welcome to Australia, stop, Gloria.' The only Gloria in the family, a relict of a long dead uncle, the sort of man who always dressed for Randwick and never had the fare to get there. My Uncle Reggie whom I never met, whom the family seldom mentioned, the black sheep. But when Gloria came to tea she brought his passport and he looked so exactly like the rest of the family and wore pince nez. 'He was a good father,' she told me loyally, 'but gambled the remittance away in the first week.' It was paid monthly, so bread was scarce most of the time.

Australia has four proud daughters, Sydney, Melbourne, Adelaide and Perth, and one son, Canberra. I used to think Sydney the pick of the girls, a bit on the tarty side, but the easiest to talk to, the best dressed, perhaps simply the most theatrical. Melbourne I found a bit of a trial, reserved, a failed debutante. But not this time; this time there was a heat wave, over a hundred most days, and the inhabitants all looking as if they had been clothed in some gigantic relief operation carried out in the dark. They had grabbed a skimpy pair of shorts, a torn kaftan, and fled the earthquake. All over the town the young propped themselves against lamp posts and desired and devoured each other. The older women seemed to have agreed on no further competition as far as hair or clothes were concerned until the weather broke.

When an Australian woman lets herself go, she goes. The scrubbed face, the curlers which never seem to be taken out, at any rate in public. Do they ever let their hair down? Are they buried in curlers? What on earth does a curler do to a woman's hair, all those hours of looking like Medusa and a brief moment of what?

This time Melbourne was beaut. Business was good too; an actor measures his appreciation of the scene against the box office returns. I met old friends, made new ones – Francis Galbally, the most eminent criminal barrister in the land. I was overjoyed, when dining with him, to have him introduce the gentleman at the next table first as the most successful columnist in Melbourne and when that proved inaccurate, insist he was a Member of Parliament, which was also apparently wide of the mark. We never did discover what he really did, but it was comforting to discover that my host, who doesn't make many mistakes, could on occasions be even vaguer than I.

124

Sydney was sticky with the heat, but a friend lent us his harbour flat for a whole month. Would you lend your flat to an actor for a month? Of course you would! Long hours in the pool, and watching from the balcony the comings and goings of Captain Cook's Coffee Cruise. Did the Manley ferries really come out from England under their own steam? I couldn't decide about Sydney this time, they seem to have spoilt it, perhaps I had never seen the slums before, but this time we played in Newtown and drove each evening from the glitter to the gloom. Those awful Australian hotels still there, those awful Australian evenings with the drunk propped against the bar. One half of Sydney keeps up with the Joneses, the other half goes down with the Kalouris, and who, you may ask, are the Kalouris? Just a family of new Australians who are finding the sledding a bit rough. They'll make out, I suppose. I hope so. But meanwhile the skyscrapers cut off the harbour view and the Dutch Royal Family send out Prince Bernhardt to preach conservation. Everyone interferes with Australia except the Australians.

Adelaide I hardly knew and this time I thought it the tops – until I got to Perth. Adelaide was brought up with a firm hand, a city a square mile in size and everything else counts as suburbs. Adelaide is the quiet one, the artistic child, the best listener, the best audience possibly in the world, so quick to get the point no one need shout. 'Let the audience do the work' has always been my creed. Here they do it without effort, they are used to theatre. I don't know why, I didn't ask, just went on gratefully every evening.

Adelaide is a family place, each vineyard producing its own wines and its own dynasty. The children go down to Melbourne to Geelong Grammar and then come home to learn the business. You might think that if your name wasn't Penfold or Hardy or Ayres it would be hard to start up, but such is not the case. You can still buy land for a song and a thousand sheep for a little more when times are bad and the rain holds off. Then suddenly the rains come and you are a millionaire if you've guessed it right. In the bush there may be no shower for five years and then ten inches of rain overnight, and you're in the flood, and what is even better, in the money.

'This,' said my younger son, who had joined us in Adelaide, 'is exactly how I pictured Australia.'

'It's not like this at all,' I told him. We were sitting on the beach, and might just possibly have been at Bognor. The children played on the sands, their parents bathed knee-deep in the waves.

'Why don't they go out further?' my son asked.

'Sharks,' I told him. In the summer, spotter planes patrol the ocean, searching out the munchies, but in the autumn it's each man for himself. Australians emphasize the drama of the bathe. Each beach has its life-savers, wearing the red hats of cardinals and arrayed in teams of four, complete with drum on which rope is coiled as we coil garden hoses. If a man or child is knocked down by the surf and carried away in the rip, they are down to the water's edge in record time, playing out the ropes to reach him. Much of the activity on the summer beaches consists of competition between the teams to see how fast they can launch each other into the waves. In Sydney they still remember with pride that the Queen Mother wore her pearls when she reviewed them. But in Adelaide the summer is spent, the life-savers have gone back to college and the munchies go unspotted.

All the same, Australia is not just beaches and bungalows, as I told my child. There is still Mrs. Ayres, thank goodness, who when she was a girl rode with her father, Kidman the cattle king, across Australia, more than fifteen hundred miles, eating breakfast before it was light and supper when the sun had gone down. In the heat of the day you didn't open your mouth unless you wore a veil. Her father owned properties galore, at one time more of the British Empire than anyone except the Crown. She remembers the ride with pleasure. Father never carried a compass, but found his way by the sun across the vast trackless bush, with thirty horses and a handful of cowboys and his two daughters. He made the damper and found the waterholes and never forgot a tree stump. He started droving at fourteen when he ran away from home after his own father had remarried, and all he took was his half blind horse.

He made fortunes in sheep and cattle and lost them in the droughts, and made them again. 'He never really liked sheep,' Mrs. Ayres told me, but he taught his children to run both. 'When sheep are bad in Australia, cattle are good' is as true today as it was then. Mrs. Ayres drove us to Victor Harbour. All her life she has wanted to see a whale out there in the bay, but the whales have gone. I kept asking her about the discomforts of her ride, but she had forgotten them. To her it had seemed a picnic, only the memory of the wild dogs still disturbed her. They had come across a bitch and her pups, set fire to the bush where they were hiding and, as they came out, the men had shot them. 'They had to do it, but it upset my sister and me.' There are no whales, no wild dogs, few kangaroos, even the rabbits are disappearing. In Victor Harbour down by the water's edge there is a monument to a tribe of Aborigines who once lived on the river bank. Mrs. Ayres remembered how on the ride they would collect the whycherly grubs and carry them in their shirts till it was time to feast. 'Did you ever eat one?' I asked, and she shuddered.

Sydney has its harbour, but also its slums, Melbourne its shops, but an uncertain climate, Adelaide its vineyards and beaches and a curious serenity. No probs, they'll tell you all through Australia. No probs, she'll be right. The dust in this happy-go-lucky land is not swept under the carpet, it just naturally collects there. In Australia nothing is ever mended until it lets in the rain. The coastline is littered with broken promises. Steps down to the beach, jetties leading to long-forgotten marinas perish and crumble away. There is no such thing as keeping up an appearance. There is no such thing as keeping up with the Joneses. There is a lunatic fringe around the Sydney Harbour where life is a society rat-race, and in Melbourne money counts, but Adelaide is a city of schools and bowling greens and uniforms; the short print dress, the dark flannels and grey blazer and then white ducks and white skirts and blue blazers when they grow up and change the school cap for the white panama and the correct club ribbon.

The temperature in Adelaide is around eighty, the water warm, the sands deserted, and the largest shark for a long time waits in the bay. Big Fred they call him, and only yesterday he savaged a fishing boat and ate a piece of the hull, or just possibly the prow. I am not a nautical man or a brave one: I shall go in just as far as my knee caps . . .

Emerging from the waves, I was confronted by two Madison Avenue-type Australians in bathing dresses, each wearing a single golden crucifix as an earring. For a moment I feared they were missionaries, but they explained they worked in the advertising department of a famous Australian store with branches throughout the continent.

'We were wondering,' they told me, 'if you were working?'

'Not at the moment,' I confessed, shaking the water out of what is left of my hair, 'but I expect to be doing so later in the day.'

'Would you consider taking on another assignment?' they askd, 'it's more or less of a temporary nature, but rewarding while it lasts.'

'That would depend,' I told them.

'We are seeking,' they explained, 'an Easter Bunny. It occurred to us you might fill the bill.'

Before we discussed money, I thought it wiser to withdraw. One can only take on a certain amount . . .

Perth had never heard of us, still hasn't. Perth is the tomboy, the most beautiful, most desirable. Here the British seem to outnumber the Aussies. On the beach I asked a fellow Pom what kept him. 'The bathing,' he told me. 'Here they have the last unpolluted ocean in the world.' I asked whether he had any desire to see the rest of the country. 'Not the slightest,' he replied, 'from all they tell me, Australia is much of a muchness . . .'

This is a dangerous country, or at least the inhabitants would have you and themselves believe so; sharks are constantly on the prowl along the beaches, the sea brings the dreaded sea wasps into the shallows to wrap themselves round the bathers. Here a man wades ashore, his shoulders covered by a curious mauve shawl, and dies on the sand; a child gets swept away in a rip and men are drowned like the late Prime Minister Holt in the surf, and their bodies never recovered. The insignificant number of such fatalities compared, say, to the toll which the traffic takes here as everywhere else, doesn't prevent the press playing each incident up for what it's worth, and a good deal more. The papers are incurably parochial, huge pictures of children off for a picnic on the shore, endless close-ups of cleavage, small rows between obscure politicians are blown up to mammoth proportions and crowd world events off front pages.

In public life the emphasis is on dullness and the spokesman inarticulate or verbose. This is a country of shirt sleeves. A man puts on a coat or turns a phrase only reluctantly. Australia seems determined not to make the best of herself, not yet anyway, the best is yet to come. No one doubts that, least of all the visitor like myself. It seems inconceivable folly that the British have deserted this huge, rich, beaut continent for the exhausted pastures of Europe. The ties are being broken, the special relationship which really existed here and never in America has almost vanished, the links that remain are become like old Christmas decorations which no one has had the time or the energy to take down for lack of a pair of steps. Australia Day, and the Governor and his Lady solemnly running up the Union Jack on the racecourse and inspecting the band as if it were a guard of honour. His Excellency speaks a few words, not bad words as it happens, but no one is listening, and why should they, when they have come to find the winner? Racing is still hugely important, betting the national pastime. Easy come, easy go, and an unemployment figure of less than one per cent. The taxi drivers here as elsewhere have tried it all before settling for a cab and a city. They have dug for gold and copper and opal; preached the Bible, rounded up the cattle; now most of them own their cabs and plan to buy another. 'Never buy a house,' one of them told me. 'A house is only somewhere for the wife to spend money. A house doesn't work for you, a second cab is different.'

Not that many of them are in the rat-race, which is run at a far slower pace here than elsewhere. This is a rich country all right; no probs. I am taken to a pub owned by the Brothers. The trade unions are very powerful and very rich. The bar was full of paid-up members and full-time officials. 'We don't go for the big strikes any more. Guerilla action is the thing, the other's too costly. Out for a couple of days, back for a week and out again. They get the message, brother.' Ask them about racial matters and they introduce me with pride to a solitary Aborigine boxer . . .

In the theatre I don't seem all that far from Shaftesbury Avenue, but I dream of adventure as I put on the slap each evening. They say in the opal mines a man still takes his life in his hands and the buyers sit in caves stashed with stones and dollars and guarded by ferocious hound dogs. Real John Wayne country, if I ever get there. I am planning to visit Ayres Rock, of course, and a fabulous dude ranch on the banks of Ross river. I am planning a trip to Hobart too, where they've opened their first casino, and then there's the Barrier Reef and surfers' paradise, and best of all Lassiter's Reef, the great gold field which Lassiter found and lost again, and which has never been relocated until . . .until . . .

I shall rename it, of course, Morley's Reef, and if by any unlikely chance I don't win the Sydney Derby Lottery, I'll be heading out west – or is it north? – pardner, for sure, with my little old pan and my little old billy can.

Me and the Maoris

It is not true that I having nothing against Wellington. I write now not, as I usually do, of the Public School I attended during my puberty but of the small, trim city nestling to the south of the North Island of New Zealand. Like Napoleon after Waterloo I fear in future I shall flinch at the very name of my conqueror.

Wellington is a city of about three hundred thousand souls, not nearly enough of whom showed up at the Opera House during the three and a half weeks I was performing my well-tried comedy *How The Other Half Loves* there. A star actor in such circumstances blames the management, the supporting cast, the lack of publicity, the draughts, the location and finally, the public. He blames the weather, the economic climate, the fact that he is preceding (or succeeding) the local amateurs, colour television, mugging on the streets, lack of public transport, absence of baby-sitters and again, the public. He never, never blames himself. It is a mortal blow to his pride ... it may also prove a mortal blow to the management's pocket, but that he can live with.

Let me say at the outset that it was never hostility I encountered, just indifference. That in my private life I was frequently hailed on the sidewalk and asked if I was enjoying myself, presented with shoes, biscuit boxes and candlesticks and commiserated with on the length of time it has been since I last visited their shores or had appeared on their screens in *Mutiny on the Bounty*. What registered most strongly in the minds of my temporary hosts was that on my first appearance in their midst, on a television programme, I confessed to not liking the local whitebait I was proffered. Normally I do like whitebait but here in New Zealand, and hardly recovered from jet-lag, it seemed unappetising. Whitebait closely resembles plankton in these parts and is not fried – but, as far as I could tell, well soaped.

What registered most strongly with me was the banner headline in the local press one evening which proclaimed: MOUSE HEAD PIE LEFT

WITH SABOTAGE LINK. Apparently the assessor was satisfied that industrial sabotage could not be excluded as the reason for the presence of the wee, cow'rin, tim'rous beastie under the undisturbed crust, but he did convict the company on charges relating to the cleanliness of the premises in question. It could happen anywhere, but mouse head pie sticks in the gullet. Of course, if the theatre had been full that night, I don't suppose I should have given the matter a thought, still less a quote . . .

'Why on earth,' I asked the captain of the Te Kotuko as we sailed the gulf of Hauraki en route for luncheon at Pakatoa Island (I trust readers will acclimatise themselves to Maori place names which begin with such confidence but fade into unpronounceability), 'does your public address system welcome us aboard with the customary insincerity of an air hostess?'

'Don't you like it?' he asked. 'The Americans like it. Sir Robert likes it.'

Sir Robert Kerridge is the legendary figure who is reputed to own most of the North Island besides being the concessionaire for all Japanese imports and the entrepreneur who, I fancy, was now slightly regretting having lured us to Auckland in *How The Other Half Loves*. It was at his invitation that we were embarked on the Te Kotuko (White Heron).

'The average passenger,' I told our skipper, 'would welcome either silence or a personal greeting accompanied possibly by a flowered lei. What fails to enchant is the disembodied voice of the tape recorder which hasn't even glimpsed the passengers, let alone liked the look of them.' I felt I had lost the Captain and, anxious that he should not get lost in his turn but steer us successfully past Motuhe Motuapo, Waiheke and The Noises (you do see what I mean), I admonished him to have a good day and returned to my seat to peruse the brochure. 'As you travel,' I read, 'the hostess will serve canned beer, spirits and soft drinks.'

Pakatoa was to prove, apparently, 'an unforgettable experience for overseas visitors and holidaymakers alike, a unique concept in holiday resorts, a holiday you will always remember.'

The voyage took about two hours and I had time to research extensively. I learned that Pakatoa is the ideal conference locale, no bustle, no pollution and no risk of delegates being distracted by outside influences. High-ho, no native dancing girls it would seem. So indeed it was to prove. When we tied up at the pier we were met by Dirk Van Dooren, a stranded Dutchman who runs the complex. Temporary residents emerged from their units and grouped themselves around the small swimming pool. It's extraordinary, when you come to think of it, how much time holidaymakers these days spend sitting on and looking at pure concrete. Lunch was laid up, as it almost always is in New Zealand. How the inhabitants managed before they found out about the smorgasbord, I cannot imagine. It is a word which covers a multitude of assorted tinned meats, beans, cold cuts and salads and the sheer inability or unwillingness of the catering staff to prepare a properly cooked meal. Together with the counter lunch, served in the hotels, which consists of fried snapper and chips, hamburgers and stewed steak, accompanied by the smell of stale oil, it is at midday the staple diet of the natives and their guests. For the dissident, however, there is often a curry to be found simmering away on a hot plate and the Pakatoa proved no exception. I helped myself twice, found it surprisingly good, and regretted having to pass up the apricot crumble. We drank flagon wine and Mr. Van Dooren, in the intervals of enquiring whether I would like to buy the place, which was apparently a gold mine Sir Robert was weary of digging, explained that the island had been purchased from the Salvation Army who had formerly run it as a home for advanced lady alcoholics. In its heyday it had a reputation for restrained hospitality, as the adjacent island of Rotorua housed gentleman alcoholics (it still does). The race that separated the islands, although hazardous, was capable of being crossed by energetic swimmers, and so successful was the cure and so invigorating the ambiance that the surf was at times alive with bathers.

I pressed our host to row over to Rotorua and have us meet some of his neighbours who in many ways enjoyed all the advantages of his own guests in search of the simple life but at considerably less expense. But it was time to return to the mainland and, as one elderly lady insisted, to the bustle and smog of the city of Auckland.

A Small Miracle in Quebec

'If the Queen came here they wouldn't dare open the door of her car.'

'In Quebec?'

'That's right.'

The speaker, as always with me, was the taxi driver. I am father confessor of all taxi drivers, to me they open their hearts. Driving round Toronto for a month, I have come to know my flock. There's the one who is married to a Japanese wife and thinks he's the luckiest man alive. There's the one who married the dame in Vegas and believes himself less fortunate. 'I'd wake up in the night and she'd be gone, with my bill fold. "Where the hell were you?" I'd ask when she got home at six in the morning. "Honey, I felt lucky and took the cab down to the Golden Horseshoe." That girl was so crazy she'd even try to sell my cab.' There's the taxi driver who is buying a house, and works days dealing with computers and nights dealing with drunks. There's the hack who has been in prison and can handle the muggers when they climb into his cab, and there's the one in Quebec who thinks they wouldn't dare open the door of Her Majesty's motor.

'Why ever not?' I asked, 'What have you got against the Monarch?'

'It's not personal, you understand. It's the money for one thing. Do you know how much she gets a year? A million and a half, and she wants a raise.'

'But you don't pay it, do you? I thought *we* paid it. Anyway, a lot of people think she pays it herself.'

'*We* pay it,' he told me, 'make no mistake, someone has to pay it, and it's us. What that dame has cost us!'

He stopped the cab outside the cyclorama of the Holy Land, a must for all good tourists. It is the largest picture in the world, was painted in 1860 in Munich and no one seems to know how it ever fetched up beside the sacred shrine of St. Anne de Beaupré. But fetch up it did, splendidly housed in a huge circular dome, and inspected hourly by hundreds upon hundreds of curious sightseers at a dollar fifty a throw. The explanation of the painting takes exactly nine minutes, and is repeated alternately in English and French, right through the day and, I imagine, far into the night. 'If you want to know who the figures are at the foot of the Cross, buy the guide book,' they tell you, 'not the Bible!'

Next door the sacred church and shrine of Our Lady was built by the traditional wrecked – or near-wrecked – sea captain who swore that if he ever got ashore again it would be to put up a church to the Virgin. There is a hospital adjacent for the cripples who come to be cured, and the enormous basement of the church is piled with crutches. I don't know what they do with them in the hospital. A very old priest was on hand to bless the faithful and selected unbelievers. I explained I had come only to shelter from the taxi driver and get a corn fixed, but he blessed me all the same. 'Did you hear,' he asked 'of the Catholic who was dying in mortal sin and when asked to say a prayer, told God he hadn't bothered him for twenty-five years and if he was allowed another twenty-five, wouldn't bother him again during that time?' I told him I hadn't, which wasn't strictly true, but as Kipling admonished us, be good to all poor parish priests.

Driving back to the city, the driver kept off the Queen and tried to get me to stop to try a piece of bread. The houses along the lake specialise in individual open air ovens and feeding the pilgrims. 'On bread?' I asked, 'just dry bread?' 'That's right.' 'No butter?' 'No butter.'

Perhaps it's the butter that is lacking in Quebec. While Toronto and Montreal forge ahead, Quebec drags her feet. She seems determined to preserve the past, to try and forget Wolfe and the final ignominy on the Heights of Abraham and remember all this was once going to be Nouveau Français, a vast continent reaching up north to Hudson Bay and down south to Carolina and the swamps of the Mississippi. In Quebec they never forget how near they were to conquering the New World. At the Laval Seminary, the largest in North America, a great map fresco on the wall reminds them of the huge, original, all-embracing parish of the Bishop of Quebec. Then we came along and spoilt everything for them, and now they only have the old town which we burnt down and the toboggan slide on the boardwalk around the citadel, and of course the Château Frontenac. The day will come, I suppose, when someone will have to start pulling that down and they will surely have to evacuate the city while he does so. It might even be cheaper and wiser to move Quebec and leave this great palace on the cliff to stand for ever as an example of what went on half way through the nineteenth century.

134

Few people realise that the Château is really not a hotel at all, but an ocean liner which no one dared to put into the water in case it didn't float. It would have done so, there can be no doubt of that, but courage failed at the last moment, and there it is high on the Heights of Abraham, looking as if a giant had assembled a do-it-yourself kit of a cabin cruiser in his back garden and found he would have to knock his house down to get it to the beach. Once inside, the illusion of being all at sea is complete; the decoration reminds one of the gay abandonment of the days when ladies and gentlemen promenaded, and Art Nouveau was indeed Nouveau. There were fishcakes for luncheon in the first class dining-room, and at tea an orchestra in powdered wigs and embroidered coats played Bach and selections from *South Pacific* in the Palm Court, while we gazed out through the stained glass portholes and tried not to notice that we were becalmed on the great waters of the St. Lawrence. Becalmed, that's the word for Quebec, and as if to drive home the point, that evening six hundred television sets in six hundred bedrooms were happily screening *Spring in Park Lane*. It was good to see Anna Neagle once more, and Tom Walls too, if it came to that.

At four in the morning I phoned the bell captain: my room had become a furnace; the radiators, long since turned off, were exploding with heat. An elderly plumber arrived and noted it was très chaud, leant out of the window and regretted there was pas de vent. Is this the evening it happens? I asked myself. Are we all to be roasted alive while the orchestra plays 'Nearer my God to Thee'? I was fairly near Him already on the very top deck of all. They gave me another stateroom and I slept fitfully, dreaming of icebergs. When I woke, the S.S. Château Frontenac appeared to be hoved to in thick fog.

Of my corn there was no trace.

Crossing the Pond

It must be forty years ago that I caught my first boat train to New York. The boat trains were specials supposed at any rate to run non-stop to Southampton Docks, although even in those days they usually stopped unaccountably just outside Brookwood Crematorium. The passengers dressed to catch them, wore orchid corsages, the extra fur coat carried over the arm, the latest novels under it. Luggage for the first class was matched and heavily labelled, the larger trunks occasionally snubbed by a sticker emphasising they were not wanted on voyage. Voyage was the word, not journey or trip. To cross the Atlantic was not only eventful, it was to follow in the trough of adventure. Great ships founder; the Titanic and the Lusitania were not forgotten; even the smaller and less significant liners carried musicians to strike up Nearer My God To Thee, should the occasion arise.

I went on the German-owned Bremen, a curious choice for Louis B. Mayer who was paying my fare, but there was an urgency about the proceedings. I was to make a film test in Los Angeles. The Bremen picked up her Southampton passengers by tender; in those days there was a mad rush to get going. It was unfashionable to be more than five days at sea, but the Bremen took six. Otherwise there was little else of which to complain, the cabins were comfortable, the food lavish and myself highly over-excited. Just to stand by the rails sharing the night with the gulls gave me a sense of urgency – so much effort to get me to the studio on time. Crossing years later on the Queen Mary, I encouraged a fellow traveller to hurl his empty champagne glass into the sea, then went to the barman and told him to be sure when the ship docked to bill my friend. My friend was tremendously impressed; he recalled it had been midnight and pitch dark with no one else about when the incident occurred, and yet in some uncanny way Cunard had realised they were a glass short. They ran a tight ship, he affirmed ever after.

Holiday camps started on board ships. We didn't have knobbly knees, but opportunity knocked at the ship's concert, and we had shuffle board and ping pong and deck quoits and bridge and horse racing and funny hats, church services and boat drill. No one shirked the last; there was a sense of responsibility aboard. This may look all right, it seemed to warn, but beware, big ships turn turtle. To don your lifejacket, to find your boat station and stand beside it, awaiting the roll call, to answer your name and wait for the ship's sirens to sound the All Clear before marching off was a chance to rehearse one's own performance in the event of the real thing happening. I was meticulous in allowing women and children to precede me, if not into the boat, for the cover remained on it, alas, at least back to the elevator. We had an elevator in the Bremen. Later, on the S.S. United States, there were no less than three elevators and bell-hops who answered the bells in the cabins and then passed on the request to the stewards. At the time this seemed the height of gracious living. It took a good deal longer to get a drink, but there was plenty of style aboard ship. Plenty of time too for romance, the clinging embrace at midnight, lovers proving to each other that seasickness was not in their make-up, that they could enjoy a force five gale together. Alas, such things were not for me. Squeamish, I always felt the slightest swell, and only with the coming of pills, invented so they said in the war to make invasion possible for G.I.s, did a feeling of drowsiness supplant the fear of throwing up over the railings.

One voyage I lay, dry of mouth but tolerably comfortable, on my bed while the ship rolled and pitched, and then suddenly I had my sea legs under me and walked up flights of stairs to reach the open sea and sky. The ship lay motionless, or what passed for motionless, in the heavy swell; the engines had stopped. Some secret rendezvous, I wondered, or had we already come further than I imagined? Was New York just around the corner, if indeed there had been the hint of a corner and not just a vast expanse of colourless sea? The ship, they told me, had buckled a plate in the storm and precautionary examination was under way. Almost at once we started again. There seemed at the time little else that we could do. I spent the rest of the voyage worrying half-heartedly about the seriousness or otherwise of buckled plates. There was always something to worry about on board ship; sudden fog, seamen's strikes, what to wear at the fancy dress ball, whether to try and improve one's cabin. One of the first and abiding anxieties was the seating arrangements in the dining room, how to ensure a jolly crowd or, as years went by, no crowd at all, and by tipping the chief steward and paying the supplement, to have one's permanent table in the verandah grill.

Once, crossing with Graham Greene and Carol Reed, we spent five days giving the children, including my own, a whale of a time, turning the Queen Mary into one vast adventure playground. There were treasure hunts and games of Sardines, and Hunt the Captain, and Flood the Cabins, and the children arrived exhausted and the rest of us thoroughly pleased with ourselves. The Customs officials came on board and because for some reason my lot were on immigrant visas, discovered that I as head of the family had defective vision, which, in the opinion of some official in London, might affect my ability to earn a livelihood. 'But you're some sort of actor, aren't you?' his opposite number enquired, just off Staten Island. 'That's right,' I told him. He tore up the document. 'Why, in your profession I reckon you're blind half the time anyway.' America was different then. Five days and not five hours different. Will they ever come back, those great ocean greyhounds, the Normandy, the Ile de France, the Aquitania? Not them, of course, but perhaps their whelps. Perhaps as the oil gets scarcer the day of the liner will return, the dinner jacket once more laid out on the bed, the bath run, the ship's news slid under the door, along with the passenger list.

Something tells me that in the plane crash I shall not have the time or courage to behave myself, but at sea with the ship slowly sinking in the fog, with the band playing, I see myself standing on the bridge, my hand raised to wish God Speed to the survivors as the boats pull away. It is true there is still one place vacant, it is also true that I am large of girth and heart. I will not add to the difficulties of the lifeboat crew, besides I am a splendid swimmer. Che sera, sera. What an actor is always seeking is an exit.

A Slice of American Pie

The one thing to avoid on holidays is the sun. Most of us have already seen it and the process of lying around, gazing up at it through smoked glasses or lying, buttock up, on damp sand or concrete patio, daring it to burn your epidermis, is not only painful but time consuming. If we feel the need to darken our skin tone, there are any number of reliable dyes on the market and the whole process can be achieved in an evening, provided no one else wishes to get into the bathroom.

No, the Costas have never been my choice. For one thing I cannot stand the anxiety of rushing to the Venetian blinds every morning to see if the blue sky is still overhead and make sure I'm not wasting my money, and for another, being a Bourbon, I burn easily. It takes me a full fifteen minutes to manipulate a beach umbrella, by which time the whole operation is useless as the sun has decided to move once more. I am happier holidaying in a land where the climate is as unpromising as it is at home and where my friends cannot fill their ears with sea shells and nod off just as I reach the point of one of my anecdotes.

I spend a good deal of my time advising Americans to visit Britain and as an inducement for them to do so I am frequently photographed – but not, alas, always distinguishable from the ancient monuments beside which I pose. Advertisers believe that the Tower of London where so many endured so much discomfort reassures, Westminster welcomes, Buckingham Palace excites. True, I suppose, up to a point, but what I believe Americans really come here for is to see the British themselves; to find love among the ruins.

That is certainly why the British, in their turn, visit America, but this year there must be a danger, which I for one am prepared to face, of being unwittingly caught up in the bi-centennial celebrations, of bumping into the Pilgrim Fathers, or a reconstruction of the Boston Tea Party, or overhearing a recording of the late Mr Lincoln. Indeed, if I go to Disney

Land, I shall make a point of the last – they have the best Lincoln since Raymond Massey. Come to think of it, it may still be Raymond Massey. Thirty years ago I remember a mutual encounter in Madison Square Garden when I followed his Gettysburg address with my, or rather Oscar Wilde's plea for the love that dare not speak its name. We were both concerned at a sudden slump in our matinée takings but Eddie Cantor, who usually compèred charity functions in those days, insisted on telling the public that our anxiety was for Munich. 'Two great Englishmen wishing they were back home,' he announced, inaccurately, over the public address system, and we got a standing ovation.

It made, alas, not the slightest difference at our respective box offices, although the war which followed soon after did interrupt my annual visit to the New York garment workers. But when I was able to return I found them as buoyant and fascinating as ever. I offered them this time a play called, *Edward, My Son*. I don't know if any of them came to it, but I spent many hours observing *them* on Broadway and 32nd Street. An ants' nest in the heart of the city, and the ants themselves all shapes, sizes, colour and authority proceeding to load, unload, fetch, carry and drop bales of identical swim suits or individually styled ball gowns amid the confusion and frustration of stalled lorries double parked, utility vans backed up by lines of traffic belching carbon dioxide and blaring klaxons. It's the frustration that fascinates, the wild improbability of the setting. We British used to be able to watch the same in Covent Garden – 'Chicken amid the Juggernauts'. But why here, one wanted to ask, why not somewhere else where there's more space to play? Now, alas, Covent Garden is banished across the Thames, but the garment workers stay put, thank goodness, and so do the potters in Santa Fe. Shop after shop filled with clay bowls and Indian bead necklaces. On one side of the track, the neon-lighted motels and on the other, the cunningly crumbled adobe arcades.

Last summer I tried the Greyhound Bus route from Vegas to New York, determined to cross the continent by Highway One, or possibly Six or Seven. I got as far as Santa Fe, listened to the weather forecast predicting snow in Denver, and chickened out. Pondering the airline time tables in the local winery, I accepted an invitation to dine with the pottery crowd, as determined a bunch of environmentally eager and anxious beavers as I have come across. Over the beans and tequila the conversation was about a mammoth bake-out to be held in the distant future. Lists were passed round with the names of the future picnickers and what each had to bring. This, I told myself, is too elaborate to be true. Sensing a more sinister explanation, I fearfully took my leave. These were not potters but plotters, I surmised, wrongly as it happened. It's extraordinary how nervous I get when suffering from indigestion.

Next morning a calmer atmosphere prevailed. I inspected the local Opera House, built for some reason in the open. My guide extended the tour to include the inevitable extinct volcano. Just above the snow belt we picked up a girl anxious to reach home before night fell. We left her at the top of the ski lift. There was no sign of habitation. 'Where do you live?' we asked, and she pointed to a mini-bus overturned in a snowdrift. 'With my friends' she told us.

'Young people nowadays,' grumbled my guide on the drive down. 'You and I have to pay for all this nonsense.'

'Surely,' I pointed out, 'it doesn't cost all that much? How many young Americans live in overturned mini-buses on tops of mountains, do you suppose?'

'You'd be surprised,' he told me.

That's why I go to America – for the countless surprises it has afforded me over the years. Opening the door to Greta Garbo, sitting in the electric chair in Sing Sing, landing my first contract at MGM and the same afternoon watching my first stick-up. Taking tea in the last private house on Fifth Avenue with the last Mrs. Cornelius Vanderbilt. Aimée Semple McPherson preaching to me and John F. Kennedy actually speaking to me. Truman Capote just looking at me, and I, of course, at him. The Hearst Ranch, Salt Lake City, The Grand Canyon, Niagara Falls, the Florida Swamps, the Earthquakes, the forest fires, Pebble Beach, Disney Land, Oscar Levant, Macy's, the World's Fair, Basin Street, New Orleans, Main Street everywhere else. Eleanor Roosevelt, Charles Manson. The good citizens. The bad. The indifferent. Like my mother used to say, 'None of us are made of sugar, we won't melt if it rains', and this year may be as good a time as ever to visit the American people. They are entitled to job back, puff out their chests and congratulate each other. They won the War of Independence, they got to the moon. What good was the moon, you ask? At least it showed willing. The problems they face today, we shall have to face tomorrow, the spin-offs of the acquisitive society. They haven't solved them, but at least they're working on them. Let us salute them all the way from Boston to Cape Canaveral, and on the way we might as well enjoy ourselves.

I should like to stop off in Washington once again, not having been there since I was junketing around the States trying to sell a book I'd written. The publisher's nanny, who travelled with me to ensure my bags were correctly labelled and that I got to the bookshops in time, had checked us in to a brand new high-rise called Watergate and, over cocktails, I met Messrs Simon and Schuster's head salesman for the territory.

'How many copies have you ordered, Bob?' enquired Nanny, and was told twenty. The fellow was obviously speaking in thousands and I felt a surge of gratitude.

'Good,' I told him. 'In New York they told me once we'd broken thirty thousand we're through the sound barrier. I'd say we'd done that now. But are you sure you're not being too optimistic . . . twenty thousand?'

'Thousands?' he answered in amazement. 'I've ordered twenty, reckon we'll sell them too, with a bit of luck.' He patted me consolingly. 'Look, kid, tomorrow you'll be on your way, but I'll have to stay around with my customers. I want them to go on trusting me.'

Next day we crossed the Potomac in the steps of General Lee and I won a great victory in Richmond, Virginia, whither I had been summoned to sign copies of the book for prospective buyers. Finding no immediate response and a pile of unsold copies, I wrote declarations of love on every fly leaf. 'One passionate night with you, my beloved, is not enough . . . Ecstasy begins for me in Richmond.' So it does. So it does.

Down Mexico Way

'Lawrence was queer?' I asked, more to break the ice than out of real curiosity.

Lowell Thomas refuted the charge vigorously. 'Not at all,' he told me, 'not in the slightest. Good Heavens, I should have spotted it at once. Later in life, possibly, but even then he had Nancy Astor on the back of his motor bike, you know.'

I asked about Aldington.

'Pure nonsense, he never met him. I went all through the campaign – the sole war correspondent and the only man ever to take the Albert Hall for a run to lecture about it afterwards. Do you know how many I turned away at my first matinée? Thirty thousand. When Lloyd George came, the Commons passed a minor vote of censure: thought he should have been in the House that evening. He was Prime Minister, you know. Of course it was only a minor vote. There are two in the British Constitution, major and minor. Did you know?'

'I know nothing,' I told him.

I had come to Acapulco as a sort of temporary rector for A.S.T.A. (American Society of Travel Agents) to install Mr. Thomas and three other distinguished Americans into the Travel Hall of Fame. The Hall is as yet unbuilt, but meanwhile there are impressive statuettes from Cartiers and an Oscar Ceremony before five thousand delegates. Not so much delegates, perhaps, as five thousand middle-aged Americans who each own small travel businesses and send their friendly neighbours scurrying around the globe. A lot of them are semi-retired; they rent an office, sometimes just a phone, and before long they're in business, 'the most wonderful business in the world. We sell pleasure, excitement, adventure, the pursuit of happiness.' It's impossible not to share their enthusiasm, not to like them. Most of all I liked the astronaut Glen Anderson walking, not hopping as I hoped, up to get his prize and explaining that all he'd done was just to open up another room.

At breakfast Lowell Thomas had asked him whether there was to be a serious attempt to explore outside our own solar system in the near future. He seemed puzzled and cautiously explained that our system was hurtling through space at eighty thousand miles an hour at present, and likely to maintain that speed for the foreseeable future. Lowell Thomas was dreaming, I think, of going on the trip and then of retaking the Albert Hall. He had been in his twenties when Bernard Shaw and Nellie Melba and most of the Royal Family sat at his feet in the dark and watched the most fascinating home movie of the day. He admitted that afterwards things had got tougher. But he was back in the saddle and riding tall, just off to the Notre Dame football match in Chicago with the Head of Notre Dame. We talked about New Zealand, where he always stayed with the Freyburgs en route to the South Pole. He shook my hand and left before luncheon, clutching his trophy.

'Strange you should have asked me that question about Lawrence,' he said, 'that was the only thing Windsor wanted to know on the telephone. He rang up himself to thank me for the flowers I sent Wallis.'

The travel agents packed, flourished their credit cards and took off, and we were left with Hotpoint and Foodland and The American College of Obstetricians. I never really discovered who the Foodlanders were, but on their last night five hundred of them sat down to a banquet around the pool, topped off at midnight by high divers and fireworks. Four hours later, the church opposite signalled the departure of the dead with massed bands and choirs and more fireworks. The dead had been here for three days, visiting relatives. They had been entertained at the cemeteries and there had been prizes for the best decorated graves. The families of the deceased had prepared elaborate meals for their guests and after a suitable wait, shared the feast. The church's icy grip on the Mexican poor is gradually being prised loose, the rapidly emerging middle class beginning to equip itself with cars and television and taking its revenge with its own package holidays. Here in Acapulco the beggars have disappeared. In Mexico City the tourist comforts himself, if not the destitute, in the belief that the Indian squatting on the pavement suckling her child is a professional, and others will give even if he doesn't. But the death rate from undernourishment is still high, despite the regular collection and inspection of mothers and children found to be homeless. The poor are frightened of the government welfare service, the government frightened of the poor. There is only a limited time before the next revolution; the students who inspired the last at the time of the Olympic Games still languish in prisons. The State does not recognise or forgive political prisoners. Political prisoners do not forgive or recognise the State.

144

Acapulco is a mindless property developers' paradise. Huge concrete hotels fringe the bay, the newest and largest has five different pools, beautifully-landscaped tropical gardens, impressive waterfalls and luxury suites at a hundred pounds a day. Not that pounds are mentioned any more than pesos, the talk is all of dollars. You may disapprove that here has been created another Miami or Vegas, but then you didn't see it before, when there was just sand and sea and swamp, and nothing in it for the Mexican who squatted by the roadside, clutching an iguana for sale that he had caught and was too poor to eat himself. Now he has work, a school for his children, enough food for them all, one day perhaps a television, even a car. It is unfortunate that civilized society offers only two alternatives to mankind, that there is no noble savage, only another little rat to join the race.

I am not a conservationist, but were I one, I suppose I should have been happier in Oaxaca, half an hour by air from Acapulco, where the ruins of Mitla and Mount Alban still wait in the sunshine for the archaeologist's trowel. Enormous, mindless stone monuments, dating from seven hundred years before Christ, built for a purpose still largely unfathomable, in exact geometric pattern, stone laid upon stone with relentless precision, unvarying, uniform and unspeakably boring. The guides drone on, explaining the inexplicable, and I wander off across the central plaza in search of shade, not easy to find seven thousand feet above sea level, and eventually sit down under a cypress tree and thank heaven there are no more stairs to climb. The cypresses – some of them are two thousand years old – what a lot of folly and unhappiness they have grown up with.

In the Victoria Hotel after dinner I saw the Englishman's idea of the complete Mexican – the blue suit, the pointed shoes, the expanse of handkerchief, the little moustache, everything just right, or wrong, depending on whether you like Michael Arlen. I was reminded of a friend who looked after actors and had about him just that air of unnatural dapperism, never a hair out of place, until one morning when he shot himself for no very apparent reason in the sunshine of Monte Carlo. It was dark in the bar, and my Mexican never let up for a moment. He danced and kissed and fondled and joked, watched all the time by exhausted culture vultures, envying him his high spirits, and just possibly his partner, and soon to wander off to bed and polish their notes and spectacles for the morrow.

We decided on an evening of folk dancing arranged by a local University Professor and after some difficulty found a small courtyard, normally part of a restaurant, where an immensely gloomy scholar was admonishing a few spectators on the pleasures to come. In the restaurant itself the diners, oblivious of the treat in store, munched solemnly, their backs to the dancers who now appeared and hopped, skipped and jumped rather carefully around, obviously aware of their responsibility to old Mexican lore. They were led, and seldom correctly followed their leader, whom I surmised to be the Professor's wife, and accompanied by a trumpeter of great talent and a small child who played on a drum slightly taller than himself, and appeared the only one to be completely enjoying himself.

We arrived back in Acapulco to find a state of emergency had been proclaimed in the elevator hall of the hotel. Huge Americans were prising open doors with crowbars and rescuing a party of their countrymen who needed oxygen and, for some reason, foot baths. We stepped cautiously around the victims, making our way to the gourmet restaurant. There was nothing we could do to help, and it was their fault for all piling in and overloading the car. After this everyone counted up to ten in the elevators and barred further entry with shrill but vehement protests. Two days later a guest fainted in the roof garden and had to be brought down, still unconscious, in a wheelchair. A small protest meeting immediately convened.

'It's sure time they fixed those elevators,' they told the outraged manager.

'The lady fainted of her own accord, she fainted on the roof, we brought her down,' he kept explaining, but like Nixon, no one seemed to believe him any more.

I confess to never feeling really well in Mexico City. It is, I think, those extra stairs leading up to the shrines and castles, and now to the new museums which seem to open up daily. They are wonderful museums, the anthropological and the modern art and the historical and the natural history, and all the others. Mexico architecturally has been for a long time now the daring young man on the flying trapeze, but although I take it slowly, reminding myself how much higher I have climbed since I left the Thames Valley, I still feel slightly sick. Not as sick as poor Mr. Kurt Vonnegut, Jnr., who was lecturing at the cultural institute with a temperature of a hundred and two. I liked Mr. Vonnegut almost as much as I liked Mr. Lowell Thomas. He spoke for an hour – a man who carefully burnt his bridges before he crossed them. Mr. Thomas had a trick of banging on his tumbler when he wished to capture the attention of his fellow diners. Mr. Kurt Vonnegut, Jnr. was not one to tap the glass, unless it happened perhaps to be a barometer. He kept his trivia to himself, but ruefully admitted it was not the weather for poets. He thought the wind would change and hoped the next generation would be able to steer a truer course, thanks to the slight adjustment he and his fellow writers had been able to make to the compass. The men who made war in Vietnam had called down on their heads the righteous anger, the burning indignation of every American novelist of the day. The effect, he told us, was that of dropping a banana cream pie five metres wide and a metre and a half thick from a height of ten metres.

At dinner a woman at an adjacent table pointed me out to her companion. 'A comedian anglais,' she remarked, 'but I do not recall the name. I do not remember them unless they are very famous,' and then proceeded to enquire of her companion whether in Taos there were cinemas. 'You're not missing much,' the old bitch remarked, when informed that there were none.

**PRIVATE
VIEW**

A Day in the Life of an Optimist

Optimism, the belief that goodness pervades reality, is like all religions, a matter of diet and environment. Avoid your loved ones at breakfast. They will only serve to remind you of how much they are costing at their various schools and how unlikely any of them are to achieve success or even financial independence. Leaving them to guzzle cornflakes and fried tomatoes, carry your own tray laden with toast, caviare, orange juice and a bottle of champagne as far away as possible. Mix the champagne and orange juice to taste, spread the caviare on the buttered toast and on no account open any letters.

There is a school of thought which permits the reading of *Country Life* along with last week's *Kent Messenger* or *Reading Mercury,* or indeed any provincial paper which concentrates on factual accounts of events in drill halls and (unless farming happens to be one's calling) livestock prices.

To congratulate oneself on missing an amateur production of *Ruddigore* or a sale of work in aid of the Cubs is permissible, indeed may be positively helpful, and there is little risk of being reminded that Richard Burton is still in the marriage market. Possibly I malign Mr. Burton, who is surely the greatest optimist of us all.

The champagne drunk, and having dedicated himself afresh, the religious will now set off for his place of work. It cannot be too often emphasised that an optimist is permitted – even encouraged – to work by his order, although mixing with unbelievers on commuter trains, especially in first class carriages, will, if he is inclined to evangelise subject him to ridicule and often violence. While the talk around him of jiggery-pokery in high places, and ineptitude, bribery, corruption on the factory floor rages; while his fellow passengers despair of the weather, grumble about the price of a decent yacht or the sum demanded at the box office for an indecent film show, the wary optimist avoids argument, closes his eyes and feigns sleep until woken by the ticket collector demanding a supplement on the third class fare he has already paid. The optimist never expects the collector.

Between ten-thirty and midday is for most optimists, and especially those who work in the City, the most testing time of the day. What is required is not only the ability to feign comfort when dressed in a hair-shirt but also some of the supreme confidence evinced by the late St. Francis whilst chatting up the birds. During these times of temptation the optimist will need all his determination not to read a balance sheet or meet an official of the Board of Trade. If he is wise he will seek the sanctuary of licensed premises and a mid-morning round of drinks whilst studying one of the most continuously optimistic of all documents – an expense account luncheon menu.

An optimist takes no thought of the caloric or cholesterol count when ordering a meal, eschewing toast melba and artificial sweeteners. He chooses oysters, asparagus, in and out of season, ground ginger, globe artichokes – anything which he has read in *Reader's Digest* or *Playboy* may improve his sexual efficiency. When he sprinkles the Chow Mein with grated horn of the white rhinoceros it is not because he is an anti-conservationist but because he may be in for an exciting afternoon.

Supreme optimists not only keep a wife but also a mistress; it is for them the red lamp of courage. Such an enthusiast will not linger over the post-prandial letter-signing at his place of work before hurrying away for tea and cakes with his beloved. In a penthouse love nest he can forget the gloomy mien of his business associates while he unwraps the chocolates and the Boucheron bauble which he has brought with him to lay at the feet of his private playmate. At this hour of the day his life takes on the added significance of the French film industry.

Most optimists, however, will not be prepared to go to such lengths to prove their ability simply to make ends meet, but will settle for the tea-time ritual of the office cup and the sweet biscuit balanced on the In-tray. They will ignore the nymphet of the trolley, concentrating as ever on the pleasures to come. It is not too late surely for the invitation to the party at the Arab Embassy? Soon they will be off in white tie and tails to the fairyland of Grosvenor Square where the diplomatic set keep their cool and an excellent table, to receive the *pièce de résistance* at the feast. Optimism, as our prophet writes, is not only in the eye of the beholder, it can also on occasion bring its own reward – the eye of the sheep.

But, of course, the invitation may never arrive. Not every evening is an Arabian night. Our optimist may be forced to go home for the evening meal long before the family are safely asleep and the danger of confrontation and domestic crisis avoided. He may even be expected to sing for his supper to the extent of reading a bedtime story, mending a light fuse or opening the telephone bill. He will rise above all these crises, supplying his own happy ending for each in turn. As he sits happily in the candlelight, a pool of confetti at his feet, his child happily asleep upstairs, finishing today's trifle or embarking on tomorrow's eggs and sausages, he will count his blessings as a miser counts his wealth. He is alive and well and living in the Thames Valley. It is true that the electricity supply is temporarily interrupted and that on the morrow the telephone will be cut off. But there is still the gas oven and the alarm clock and his unshakable belief that good ultimately predominates over evil in the world.

It is time for our hero to grope his way up the stairs, undress in the dark and climb into bed, to fall into a dreamless sleep. He has, after all, nothing left to dream about.

Accustomed as I am to Public Speaking . . .

'How would you like,' they ask, 'a trip to Acapulco to give away the awards to the International Balloonists' Association?'

'Very much,' you tell them, and wait expectantly.

'A round trip ticket – first class, naturally – for two?'

'For two!'

'And hotel accommodation and a solatium?'

Once it has been decided to have a conjuror it is always a problem to fix the fee. 'How much would you think was reasonable?' they ask. With balloonists the sky is the limit, you imagine. They laugh uneasily. A figure is broached. You're up and away. It's as simple as that.

At the other end of the scale is the Christmas Bazaar – a humble affair miles from Acapulco, miles from anywhere – on the way to Friern Barnet. No solatium, only the vague hope you will be doing your bit for the Retired Lighthouse-Keepers' Fund. They need that little extra at Christmas now they've left the lighthouse and no helicopter ferries in the turkey and plum pudding.

I never really enjoy opening bazaars; if people decide to support the cause they leave it till later, round about three. Bazaars are opened sharp at two – just the stall-holders, the lady who rang you up last August and her husband playing the Mr. Thatcher role and anxious for you to know he is usually busy in the afternoons. I tell everyone that it's great to be asked on this great day to help this great cause. And that I haven't had to do all the hard work (that bit's true, at least), and I'm not going to detain them a moment longer from spending their money. Then I progress round the stalls spending my own. A cake here, a duster there, and home-made chutney. At least you are sure of the chutney . . . it is impossible to have a failure with chutney; there's nothing to set and no ingredient barred. As I leave the public starts to arrive. Do they realise they've missed me? Have they missed me? If so, they are putting a brave face on it; at this sort of function you need a brave face right through the afternoon.

Acapulco, of course, is more fun – more rewarding too. The vast junket is sponsored by the people who make the balloons, who bottle the gas, who construct the baskets. There are any number of side-shows besides myself. The town is full of conventioneers wearing perspex identity labels; if they were all struck dumb or suffered heart attacks or lost their memories they could be instantly packaged and returned to Washington, Wyoming, Hot Springs. My badge is usually a little more elaborate than theirs – the rosette larger . . . should one wear it at all? It's like announcing one's own name on TV commercials – if they don't know who you are, to hell with them. But of course a lot of them don't know who you are and never will. You can see their lips moving as they spell out the label – at least it's printed clearly. When you give them an autograph you leave them trying to make out who the devil Rob Mosspy thinks he is.

Your part in the ceremonial parade may take only a few moments; once you've made your speech, given away the prizes, you are no longer an employee; you sign for the steak dinner; in an altogether more lordly manner you accept congratulation, your ticket home and your solatium. You tell everyone how much you've enjoyed it and are promised, by a slightly optimistic PRO, a return date next year. You never quite know what to do with the shrunken head they gave you on that last evening. Could it have been a hint? But surely you were asked to show off? Only when you learn that next year's guest is to be Alice Faye do you dispose of it.

Between Acapulco and Friern Barnet come the public luncheons, the banquets, the Brains Trusts, the debates, the invitations to drop in and draw the lucky number out of the tombola. It is never wise to arrive early at any of these functions; once the organisers have got it into their heads that you are going to let them down and not show, they are extravagantly grateful when you finally do turn up. The gin fairly splashes into the glass – it is easy for you to play the hand outstretched. 'But you couldn't really believe I'd forget this was the day? I've been looking forward to it for weeks. Tell me who everyone is.' My trouble is, I can never remember who they are for ten seconds. I confuse the Chair. with the Sec. and mistake last year's Pres. for this year's Treas. Luckily, there are a few simple and abiding guide lines. Everyone works hard at an extraordinarily difficult job, finds immense satisfaction in their task, can be persuaded to tell you at some length how they came to join the organisation, who came to the party last year, and whether or not they've seen *Billy* at Drury Lane.

At luncheon it is always much more difficult to talk to men than women. Although I have a sneaky admiration for their love of punishment

I personally find the Rotarians something of a trial. For one thing, they usually ask me to speak about the theatre – about which they have a very limited knowledge and interest – and for another the food is always terrible. I think food is important, obviously, but never more so than shortly before you are due to be spoken to – or should it be at?

Years ago I campaigned in Australia for a higher standard of public nosh. After I had been asked out on at least fifty occasions and invariably complained about the quality of the cold ham, I was bidden to a special banquet and invited to choose the menu. I suppose I went to town, but on this occasion I was the only one to be served with caviare, sole and a partridge – everyone else ate ham as usual. I think I was supposed to feel ashamed, but I didn't – just not as hungry as usual.

Nearly everyone who rises to propose a toast begins by depreciating himself or herself, saying how unfit they are for the task and how worried their spouse or child is at this moment in time. The battle is lost before it's begun but you can't stop them going on trying to fight it. Hence the nightly torture inflicted on all good men foolish enough to come to the aid of the party.

There is another side of the business I haven't touched on but which provides a golden retirement to a host of charming and unobtrusive busybodies who flit from Angmering to Broadstairs and back to Luton, speaking at Ladies' Luncheon Clubs on everything under the sun from cleaning the Crown Jewels to keeping bees in the Holy Land. Such activity is organised by professional matchmakers who have an encyclopaedic knowledge of their clients' depth of interests and purses, who select from their catalogue of playmates the one most likely to succeed at a party of culture vultures in Basingstoke and who will leave their listeners a little wiser and better briefed on the loves of the late Lord Byron. It is not knowledge which will stay with them. There is no danger that next week their thoughts will still be on Marathon when they are finding out exactly what to do to get a reasonable brass rubbing when they've forgotten the blanco. Knowledge comes and goes, and there is no lack of speakers. One of the really nice things about talking to the girls is that you get the fee immediately afterwards in a plain envelope.

In Praise of Strikes

When is a strike not a strike? In my book, the Random House Dictionary of the English Language, eighty-five times out of eighty-six. The forty-first usage of 'to strike', however, is given as 'to leave off work, or stop working as a coercive measure, or as at the close of day'. As a cowardly man, I flinch from the other eighty-five definitions. I am in favour of leaving off work at the close of day, earlier if possible. I have never been able to work myself up about the folly and wickedness of industrial action, any more than I have been able to excite myself about the economy, the balance of payments or the growth rate of industry or the human race.

The classical dilemma of the worker is that, while it is boring to go on, it is equally boring to stop altogether. The solution, therefore, is to stop for a breather, hence the popularity of strikes. If a man works at a job which totally bores him, life itself becomes meaningless and his world a treadmill. A blue sky, a cold sea, a slippery slope, a desert, an oasis, a hill, a valley, an island, a continent, each is unobserved by him. In a world in which men come in all shapes and sizes, in which no mould is ever repeated, except in the case of identical twins, in which no two views are ever alike, the colour of each blade of grass differs one from the other, and every pebble on the beach is separate and distinct; such a man, his eyes shut tight, his lips pursed, his ears deafened, is engaged in the task of car spraying, taking pains that every car should look as much like the last as possible, defying Nature, defeating himself. Such a man should lie down and be carried off on his own assembly line.

Man, unlike the animals, has never learnt to understand or appreciate his environment. The best times are had by butterflies and bears; possums are happy, but not man. Cats are content, but not man. I never think dogs are happy, but that is perhaps because I am never happy with them. Pheasants look happy, but not the Duke of Edinburgh when he is trying to shoot them. Mention of pheasants reminds me of the saddest of all sitting ducks – the Secretary Bird. There can be few more depressing human predicaments than to sit for hours on end, listening to business men calling to one another, or to have to perpetuate the banalities of commercial correspondence on crisp notepaper with a carbon copy beneath. In our society, battery hens are more kindly treated than audio-typists.

Which brings me to my point: the best of all possible strikes is the Postal Strike. Letters have brought me little happiness in the past. The ones I have written were largely a waste of my time and effort, the ones I received scarcely worth perusing, let alone preserving. I don't say I haven't experienced an occasional warm flush over the panegyrics of a fan from Bournemouth, but equally I have experienced despair over a communication from my bookmaker. I have written a good deal of nonsense, and read even more. I have endured the flattery of investment advisers, the ravings of religious fanatics, the ceaseless admonitions of accountants. I have wasted months of my life turning the pages of the catalogues of art dealers, silversmiths, Dutch bulb growers, department stores and makers of burglar alarms. There are times when it has seemed to me that no church fête could take place up or down the country without an appeal to me to send an article of personal apparel, or a thumb print. Why should a man who is willing to pay half-a-crown to help restore an eighteenth-century pulpit in Blackburn be lumbered with my signature scrawled on a postcard? It would be marvellous to wake up and realise one cannot possibly receive a personal appeal from Lord Louis Mountbatten or Peter Scott, nor find that one has been selected by the *Reader's Digest* as a recipient of its largesse.

When at last, unable to resist the entreaties of my fellow citizens any longer, I am dragged in token reluctance to the seat of power, I shall make it a criminal offence for anyone to possess a typewriter, to dictate a letter or write to someone they do not know personally. I shall also make it mandatory for all workers to strike for at least a month each year. The public will have the excitement of a milkless month, a meatless month, a lawless month, a paperless month, a televisionless month, and so on. It will be able to break the monotony of the Sunday joint and the daily pinta and recapture for itself temporarily at any rate the pleasures that it has forgotten − candlelight, exercise, silence, conversation. It will learn independence and commonsense once more.

Out of the Mouths of Babes . . .

Late December, early January is the time when most people can get a New Year if they want one. Most people don't. They grumble a good deal about their present model, they pretend to be delighted with the prospect of the new one, but in the end they decide to make do with what they've got already. 'Why bother to change?' they ask. 'There's sure to be teething troubles. Then again, supposing we did get a New Year, would we be able to drive it?'

I asked my year-old grandson whether he thought I ought to get a Happy New Year.

'It depends, I suppose,' he told me, 'what sort of New Year you want – a good resolution New Year?'

'I'm absolutely sick of those,' I told him. 'Besides, they don't work.'

'A year of endeavour, perhaps?'

'That's a bit vague. What sort of endeavour?'

'This could be the year when you took over, came to power, ran the country.'

'Yes,' I told him, 'that would be quite nice.'

'It would mean a lot of work.'

'But I don't mind work as long as it's interesting work. That's why I'm so grateful I don't have an assembly line job.'

'I expect they're grateful too,' he observed. He seemed to be having difficulty balancing his bricks. I tried to give him a hand, but for some reason he bit it.

'If you ran the country, what would you do?' he asked.

'Certainly get rid of the slums.'

'How?'

'It's perfectly easy to get rid of things. I'd just knock them down, like you do.'

'And meanwhile, where would people live?'

'They could live in huts. If there were an earthquake, they would have to live in huts.'

159

'How about their coming to live here?'

'What, all of them?'

'Some.'

'It wouldn't do, wouldn't do AT ALL!'

'There's no reason to shout. You're the one that's deaf,' Hugo reminded me rudely.

'Let's forget the slums for a moment,' I went on. 'There's the question of unemployment. That's something I could deal with. I should adopt the Japanese system. In Japan when a firm takes on an employee it assumes an obligation. It looks after him and his family for the rest of their natural.' Hugo flinched: he is opposed to slang. 'In Japan,' I continued, 'they believe in jobs for the boys.'

'So do our lot,' said Hugo.

'But this is entirely different. There, all the school leavers are automatically absorbed. It's a point of honour for employers to take them on, even if at the moment they don't need additional staff. They never sack anyone. Once an employee, always an employee, unless you are criminally dishonest, and even then they will try and save your face for you, if not your job. In Japan losing face is very tragic, which is why no one calls anyone a bloody fool.'

'The British,' sighed Hugo, 'like sacking each other and calling each other a bloody fool.'

'Yes, and look at the economy. Bad labour relations, that's the trouble.'

'If you had your way, would you sack the present government?' asked Hugo.

'Yes.'

'Why?'

'Because they're a lot of bloody fools.'

Hugo seemed to have arranged the bricks to his satisfaction. 'What would you do about the trade gap and sterling as a reserve currency?'

'Absolutely nothing – it's only book-keeping. I've never kept accounts. It's a mistake to put down what one spends, or to add up what comes in. Just be grateful for the stuff when it's around. I had an uncle, well, you had a great-great uncle, come to that, who used to put down every penny. On his deathbed he asked me whether I'd taken a taxi or come by bus to get to it. I thought it the saddest thing anyone ever asked. How could it matter, then or ever? He was the kindest of men, too, in some ways.'

'Leave you any money?' Hugo asked me.

'He did, as a matter of fact.'

'I wish you would keep accounts,' said Hugo, 'It might be a help to all of

160

us. But go on with what you were going to do if you ran the whole caboodle.'

'It's quite simple,' I told him. 'I would get the country on its feet, get the economy moving.'

'Everyone,' said Hugo, 'always wants to get someone else up on their feet. It might help if you got up on your feet a bit more yourself, instead of slumping in your chair all day, watching the television.' He rose, I thought a trifle unsteadily, and tottered in my direction. Then he sat down abruptly.

'Hard luck, old fellow.'

'What do you mean, hard luck?'

'You didn't quite make it.'

'I had a partial success. In her present mood, Great Britain might argue that I also had a partial failure, but I prefer to ignore that aspect. I travelled three steps; tomorrow or the day after I shall walk right across the room. Then in a few weeks across the garden, then in turn across the street, and the town, and the country, and the whole wide world. Why? Because instead of commiserating with myself for what I haven't achieved, I continue to congratulate myself on what I have. That's the difference, and try to remember it in future.'

'I'd like to congratulate you,' I said.

'Why me especially?' asked Hugo. 'If you want to congratulate anyone, congratulate the entire human race, and especially the human race between the ages of one and five. That's the testing time.

'Why do you wrinkle your nose up like that?' I asked.

'Because I smell success.'

'I wish I could,' I told him.

'You have to sniff for it. It's there more often than you might suspect. It's one hell of a sweet smell.'

I was surprised at Hugo's vehemence. He hardly ever swears. One of his attendant slaves came to collect him and carry him off to his bath. At the door he turned and waved gravely.

'A Happy New Year,' he said, 'and mind you sniff for it.'

Waste Not, Want Not

Each morning I pad down to the kitchen and while my wife lays up the breakfast tray, I pick up the mail from the floor and tear open the envelopes. On an average half of their contents go, after a moment's hesitation, into the dustbin outside, although for some reason I am usually left with the envelopes. I realise that a good deal of time, effort and thought has gone into the task of contacting me in favour of the *Reader's Digest's* special offer of *The Tale of Two Cities*, or to alert me that a limited number of medals are now available (but won't apparently be so for long) with Churchill's face on the obverse. I don't, of course, believe that just because *I* don't rise to the bait, no fish are caught that particular morning. It's true I have never seen a Churchill medal on the lapel of any of my neighbours, but we are an unostentatious lot around this neck of the Thames Valley. It is not for me to estimate how much it costs someone to employ the vast army of executives, market experts, typists, designers and even postal sorters to mount these operations, but it must pay, and life would be immeasurably duller if people like me were not apprised daily of an entirely new scheme which would cut out death duties, or of another which will enable us to make a profitable living on the racecourse in future.

I only mention all this because on my desk at this moment there lies an order form for an article of six hundred words on Waste, numbered Job No. 062J503, and promising a reward. I should have been annoyed if it had found its way into the dustbin.

When chided that I am wasting time, money or breath, I am fairly certain to be enjoying myself. I am not so much a waster as a recylist. I recycle money at speed, in at one pocket, out the other is my practice. No one knows how long the stuff will last; the trick surely is not to be caught holding any of the bread when you are picked up for the last time. I wasn't even holding any when I was picked up for the first time, unless you count one or two pre-birth rattles and a small sum payable on my twenty-first birthday, a legacy from a defunct grandparent. Even when you are a baby it is never wise to count on anything promised from living relatives. Where there's a will, there is often a change.

Spending and money are synonymous — like moment and time. I am not saying it's a waste of breath to utter such phrases, because some people enjoy using redundancies, and the whole idea of saving one's breath is ludicrous. The quickest way to die is to hold your breath, or get someone to hold it for you. I suppose if someone really bores you, you might ask him to recycle his breath a little more slowly, but it probably wouldn't help in the long run, which brings us to the third imponderable, Time itself. Nearly everyone resents the other fellow's work rate. The man in the Jaguar will honk at the roadmender, brewing up; the housewife chivvy and complain of the plumber who is taking time out for a fag. The housewife genuinely believes it's her time because she is paying for it. Victorian tyranny subscribed to the theory of time being bought and sold. A twelve-fifteen hour day was not uncommon. Later ten, and now eight hours is regarded as the acceptable norm. Doctor Brudski, the celebrated Polish economist (who resides, naturally, in London) recently opined that a four-hour day would soon be mandatory if the economy was to recover equilibrium, and I go along with the doctor. Personally, I enjoyed the recent three-day week. I didn't work it, actually, because I wasn't employed at the time, but I know a lot of people who did. Thursday to Monday makes a nice break. '*You* may have enjoyed it,' my business friends tell me, 'but we lost a hell of a lot of motor cars and pocket computers.'

Pocket computers are the new growth industry, apparently. I bought mine in the transit lounge in Bahrein, because all the sales staff were using them avidly. It now lies in a drawer of my desk, along with tape recorders, pocket barometers, desk sets, electric erasers, complimentary money clips, jumbo-size fountain pens, eight rulers and three travellers' cheques for twenty pounds each. I think I shall probably throw away a ruler one day soon, but I don't imagine even then it will be wasted. Some fool is sure to unearth it eventually on the rubbish heap, and take it home. 'Look what I've found,' he'll tell them, 'a perfectly good ruler.'

It's easy to get rid of money and time and breath, and typing paper, come to think of it, but rubbish clings to one. If all the cardboard boxes containing old lampshades were collected and piled on top of each other, and a man climbed to the summit of the heap, he could look down on Everest.

It is More Blessed to Receive . . .

The last time I saw Tokyo, from a bedroom on the seventeenth floor of what was in those days the Tokyo Hilton, I watched from the window an apparently endless procession of exquisitely-wrapped Japanese ladies bearing exquisitely-wrapped gift packages through a side entrance of the building reserved for wedding receptions. I asked what the packages contained and was told sugar. The Japanese have always been ahead of the rest of us. How sensible, how time-saving is a convention which cuts out all those hours agonising between fish slicers and fruit bowls!

What is needed by package tourists and travelling salesmen is some similar convention which decrees that the returning traveller should carry the ritual gift prescribed for such occasions and absolutely nothing else. A pair of gloves or a posy of artificial flowers never intended to be worn or sniffed and capable of being re-donated and instantly returned by the recipient. If custom ordained that such gifts should be presented at the airport they would have to be included along with passport and vaccination certificate on the outward journey, but it would be more convenient, surely, to keep them in a drawer at home and parade them ceremonially when one was home and dried.

Whether we like it or not we are leaving the world of A PRESENT FROM MARGATE tastefully engraved around miniature chamber pots. A check of the dressing-tables, mantelpieces and window ledges in my own house revealed no less than seventeen different pieces of vertu readily associated with such widely-scattered fun spots as Folkestone, Acapulco, Sandown (the Isle of Wight, not the racetrack), Catalina Island, Stratford upon Avon, the Tivoli Gardens, Copenhagen, Burton upon Trent, and Niagara Falls. One particularly crowded parking lot in the sitting-room is at present utilised by a Delft china windmill, a silver spinning-wheel, a cuckoo emerging from an ivory egg (tasteful stuff this, brought back as a gift to myself from Hong Kong), a folding mirror from Palma, cocktail swords from Toledo, a cuss box from Torquay, and the Eiffel Tower masquerading as a thermometer. Scattered around are Spanish hats, Indian jewelled elephants, camel saddles from Morocco, and a Chinese coolie costume which my daughter, who returned with it from South Africa only the other week, thought might come in handy.

These are, of course, only the tip of the iceberg, just the trophies we have acquired lately or haven't had the courage to dispose of as yet. Heaven knows how many useless and unacceptable gifts we have distributed to unoffending members of our family and circle. 'So sorry we couldn't take you with us to Madeira,' we tell Auntie on our return, 'but this is a genuine replica – in miniature, of course – of the kind of sleigh they use to come down the hill just outside Funchal.' From the moment she holds it in her hand she is uncertain what to do with it next. How grateful both of us would be if a stop could be put to the nonsense, the last two or three days of the holiday not spoilt by the shopping. Forsaking the beach and bistro and cutting out the after-lunch brandy, we drag ourselves around in the heat pricing handbags, shawls and leather flagons of undrinkable wine. There is no country left in the world which does not specialise in leather work, glass work, copper work. The whole world glints with saucepans.

Worse still, there has been a recent migration of indigenous rubbish. Thus, Eskimo carving is on sale throughout Canada and pre-Columbian bric-à-brac parades itself shamelessly on Bond Street and Madison Avenue. No one rash enough to purchase a Bolivian church bell in situ can be certain it wasn't cast in Stockport. A good deal more is made in Japan than meets the eye in Osaka.

I have never subscribed to the myth that it is the thought that counts. With me it's the gift every time and in choosing what to bring back on such occasions I favour the consumable – scent, wine, joss sticks, salami, shark fins – as opposed to the durable – beads, ships in bottles, papier-mâché, pill boxes, animals stuffed in their own fur, and cheap – and, for that matter, expensive – cuff-links. If I *have* to go into the durable market I select sponges, laundry baskets, pool sweepers, coins in plastic cubes and executive desk toys. I know I can buy such things at home but somehow I never seem to spot them except in Abercrombie and Fitch. I once returned with a genuine Japanese pachinko machine as a present for the grandchildren. A great success. I still have it. You simply cannot buy them in this country and now ten years afterwards people ask me where I got it. Boy, that's prestige!

Normally I avoid shopping in transit lounges, but in a Bahrein boutique I recently purchased, for reasons still not clear to me, an instant computer capable, or so I imagined at the time, of multiplying thirteen to infinity. I set about my task with one ear cocked to the public address system – I wasn't proposing to be there all night– and almost at once the magical screen packed up. The nines predominated and tended to endure. I hastened back to the counter and with a smile which clearly said 'You picked the wrong guy, chum', held out the machine and the receipt. The salesman gave in without a word, ripped a new computer out of its cardboard box and handed it over. It just shows, I told myself, the state of the computer market. There could easily be an epidemic of poisoning among pocket calculators involving the whole Middle East. No wonder oil is costing so much.

My worst fears were confirmed when, after a few manoeuvres, this one also stuck, and at the same moment the flight was called. Back in my safety strap I sulked.

'You should not,' I told my hostess, 'allow innocent passengers with travellers' cheques loose in transit lounges. I have been conned.' I held up my purchase and she took it from me and deftly set it to work.

'You don't,' she told me, 'know how to use it. As soon as I've taken round *The Gulf Times* I'll come back and teach you.'

It's still working fine. I never use it, but it's still working. Pocket calculators are, come to think of it, the ideal gift for returning travellers, they have built-in play value. They amuse and stimulate far longer than jade buffaloes, book markers, miniature bottles of schnapps, and old motor car horns. They are more useful and only a shade less decorative than Burmese temple bells, carved ivory or Arab gongs. They are not, of course, preferable to the jug I came across recently in a top cupboard. A real find, I fancy. This exquisite piece of old china bears a picture of a small boat passing under the cast iron bridge over the river Weare which was begun by R. Burdon, Esq. on September 26th 1793 and opened on August 9th 1796. The jug apparently commemorates the return not only of the vessel, but of Henry and Jane Davidson of Monkseaton, who sailed in her in 1848. Someone thought fit to inscribe it as follows:

> Thou noble bark of brightest fame
> That bears proud England's honest name
> Right welcome home once more.
> Welcome, thou gallant little sail,
> In England's name I bid thee hail
> And welcome to our shore.

166

Repetitious, possibly? Valuable – ah, who can tell? I might just be persuaded to part with it. Perhaps some honest dealer reading these lines will tell himself, and possibly me, that I have in my possession and in pristine condition the Monkseaton jug, the only other known copy of which is in the Getty collection, and invite me to state my price. Which is why I have ended this chapter as I have done.

How to Increase Your Worry Potential

Sitting in the Tsar's box at the Khirov last week (hold it, Morley), and watching a contemporary opera about Peter the Great (nearly everything in Leningrad is about Peter, who built the place) I was disturbed by a movie camera exactly behind my left ear. If there are to be pictures, I prefer to face the lens. Moving my seat in the interval I found my neighbour to be a Washington economist in Russia to advise the Soviets on matters relating to communication costs. Anxious to disguise my incredulity and engage in appropriate banter, I opined that the Soviets would be foolish indeed to take a leaf out of America's book at a time of full employment in the U.S.S.R.

'The economic situation over here,' he assured me gravely, 'is not without its problems.'

'You could have said the same about Britain,' I told him, 'a few weeks ago, but by now I am sure we will have solved them.'

Imagine my surprise, therefore, when arriving home I found the press and politicians still as deep in the wood as ever. There seemed to be no European investors searching in the financial jungle for the British Babes. However, almost as soon as I set foot on home ground, I heard on the wireless that everyone – or nearly everyone – was to be given another six pounds a week to be going on with. The extraordinary thing to me is that we British are still worrying about inflation, until you realise that without something to worry about life cannot go on in this country. I have long wanted to compile a treatise on the best method to increase worry potential and thereby raise the sum total of contentment among my fellow Britons.

At least recently in Britain we have all taken a great stride forward and learnt to concentrate on worrying solely about money. We are unquestionably better worriers than our parents. During the two last wars there was nothing like the same volume of worry generated about the final result – indeed it was considered rather bad form to contemplate an

168

unfavourable outcome to the contest. A slogan of one of our late monarchs was adopted as a sort of national password. True, she pronounced her dictum more than half a century before, in a completely different context, but many thought it would be all the better for that. We came through before, why not again? Thank goodness that sort of thinking is unfashionable. We not only contemplate the possibility of defeat, we insist upon it. We no longer remind ourselves that we are British and usually come out on top; on the contrary, our politicians never cease comparing us unfavourably to South America, a country which has always served them as a convenient bogey land.

Indeed, in the days when we permitted our worries to roam far and wide there was always the faint anxiety that our sisters, on a shopping expedition and unaccompanied, might feel a sudden sharp sting in the arm and wake up in a Buenos Aires brothel. Just as it is difficult for the human being to feel two pains simultaneously, he is incapable of worrying about two different things at the same time. In concentrating on the country's financial plight, we British have rid ourselves of worrying about the weather (and how right we were last summer), our national health (better as doctors work shorter and shorter hours), whether people still like us (they don't), and what is to become of our children (never mind the kids just at the moment, let's get on with the overtime while it's still around).

Inflation is now the sole topic of conversation, and what a welcome change it makes from all the nonsense people used to talk about the theatre or music or literature. No one ever asks if anyone has read a good book lately, what he wants to find out is how the pound did after trading hours on the pavement bourse. He is not actually thinking of changing pounds, but of telling us a story of his student days in Grenoble when the entire holiday cost him two pound ten for a fortnight, including yodelling lessons from a Swiss milkmaid. 'Do you know what it would cost today?' he asks, and has the answer ready before we are . . . Seven hundred and fifteen pounds sixty pence, and for that of course there would be no question of individual tuition.

Gone is the bore who, when arriving for lunch, couldn't wait to tell us of the route which cut out the Staines bottleneck; in his stead we have an entirely new bore – well, very nearly new – asking before we have poured the gin if we can tell him what they ask for a car wash these days in the Fulham Road?

I am happy for my fellow countrymen that at last they have learnt to speak to each other in railway carriages about how much they've paid for their tickets, that they crowd into restaurants not merely to eat but to find

169

out how the price of Lobster Newburg or Tripe à la Façon de Caen has risen since the same time yesterday, and to tell us it tomorrow. 'Expenditure,' in the memorable phrase of Doctor Pollinge, the celebrated Sikh economist, 'is the grease on the axis of the inflationary spiral; without grease the gyroscope falls off the string.' So we had better be careful. Without inflation we should have nothing whatever to discuss or to think about. 'What will happen,' we used to ask each other, 'when the war is over? What will they find to write about?' We needn't have worried.

But suppose, just suppose, that the magic of giving everyone an extra six pounds really worked and prices tumbled and the pound rose and useful and meaningful occupation was restored to all men and the assembly lines started up again at twice the speed and office blocks sprouted and the air was filled with Concordes. That this country became once more the Hub of the Universe, that the Empire and the Colonies were ours again, not by conquest this time, but just because men saw that only if they marched in step with Britain could they travel in the right direction. It would not be so much the demand of foreigners, 'Take Us to Your Leaders,' as 'Send Us Your Leaders', and off they would go on a lap of victory while we British sat back once more in the lap of luxury. Well, I mean, there's no harm in supposing.

Where There's a Will

It is extraordinary how seldom I ever make wills. I take a vicarious pleasure in the stories of dustmen who have taken pains to bury old ladies' gin bottles in their back gardens and are rewarded by being left their fortunes. 'She would come into the shop sometimes, and we would have a bit of a chat, but I never dreamt she was worth all that, and that she would leave it to me,' says the delighted village postmistress when the eccentric dog-breeder down the road suddenly snuffs it. Of one thing I am sure: it's no good being too close if you want to inherit. Everyone longs to spring a surprise at the last, even if they can't be there to watch the fun.

I have a particular aversion to the poetic flummery which leaves everyone the sky at morning or birdsong at night or the corn ripening in the meadow, and then gets down to the nitty-gritty and discloses there's no estate worth mentioning. On the other hand, I am fond of the quirky testator who plans to leave his millions to as yet unconceived heirs, on condition his daughter's husband has nothing whatever to do with the fur trade and has never ridden a horse.

I like the idea, too, of beneficiaries having to change their name, or better still, add a hyphen and go double-barrelled if they want to inherit. 'In future Mr. Tom Jones wishes to be known as Mr. Tom Bardslay-Jones' – *wishes*, indeed! Why not say straight out it's either that or goodbye to fifteen thousand?

Literature about wills always delights me. There's that unlikely play by Barrie in which the couple keep changing their intentions and end up with no one to leave the money to anyway. Then there is the whodunnit in which the family gathers at midnight at Aunt Tabitha's, whose testamentary intentions are not disclosed until the last victim is found in the rock garden, bludgeoned to death with a flower pot. In fact, as in fiction, Aunt Tabitha outlives them all. In these days of death duties and possible wealth tax, a will no longer matters as much as it did to the next generation. Keep in touch, certainly, but don't hang around should be the

171

guide in these more realistic times. Both my grandfathers tied their money up in quite complicated wills, and my father, who was usually in need of the ready, was forever thinking up ingenious ways of getting his hands on some of it. I remember his ecstasy on being once informed by a new solicitor he had engaged to assist in the task, that there had never been an entail yet through which the fellow could not drive a coach and horses, given a little perseverance. Father delighted in the phrase; he had been a notable coachman himself in his day, but I don't think the solicitor delivered the goods because he was dismissed after a time, and Grandfather's money went where he had intended, more or less.

I had an uncle whom I used to vex a good deal by taking taxis when he thought I should travel by bus, or better still, walk to visit him on his deathbed. He was not a mean man, but spending money made him unhappy, and to watch others spend it saddened him immeasurably. He left a small fortune, of which the government took their share, and I thought how much more fun he would have had spending the stuff, but of course he wouldn't have. There are the savers and the spenders, and woe betide us when the balance is faulty. Uncle left me ten thousand and I spent it quite easily in no time at all: he wouldn't have expected anything else. People live on a plateau of money from which they seldom stray; a man hard up for fifty at twenty will be hard up for fifty all his life, allowing of course for inflation. On the other hand there are people like myself who are hard up for a bit more than that. If you remove a man artificially, say by leaving him a million, from one plateau to another, he may not survive, although I have a friend who spent his youth in comparative penury, always hoping to buy a car, then his father died and left an undertaking business to a brother, who died in his turn, intestate. 'Ask me,' my friend demanded next time we met, 'how many cars I have now.' I obeyed and he told me he had twenty-seven Daimlers to follow the hearse and a Jaguar for himself to pass it on the road.

I am at the age when obituary columns make news. I look in *The Times* and find the name of an acquaintance I thought was still around and now obviously isn't, and ask myself whether perhaps he has left me something. There's no earthly reason why he should; the chances must be a thousand to one against, but I like the long shots. I browse in the bath, hopes as high as the water going out the waste pipe. There's always a chance, just as there is the chance that I may be remembered by a loyal matinée fan or even a distant relative in Australia. Whatever happened to all those wealthy Australians who used to return loaded and cut up for millions? Did they only exist in Act III of the plays we used to go to? I had another uncle in Australia, and one by marriage in Canada. Of course they've been dead for years, but posts are very slow nowadays and so, come to think of it, are executors, unless of course you choose your bank manager. Why not go along right now to see him about the disposal of your earthly goods, and it might be a nice idea to leave me a little for the suggestion.

As Chance Would Have It

I wish I understood Providence. We do not meet, alas, as often as I would wish, and always so unexpectedly.

The other evening at Doncaster, for instance. Five nights earlier we had missed each other at Wolverhampton. I can quite understand Providence not showing at Wolverhampton. In the days when I was on tour in the provinces most of the year, Monday to Saturday twice nightly at the Grand Theatre, Wolverhampton, was enough for me. If there was a midnight train after the performance, I was on it.

I only visit the city peripherally these days to inspect the race track. Even so, disaster usually strikes. It is not an easy track to find. Nearby, the notorious Spaghetti Junction lies in wait for victims. So awesome is this complex of motorways, so complicated its maze, that a driver can become entangled in the web and, with tears blurring his vision, and his windscreen wipers at full tilt, he has to wait to be rescued by expert trackers and seldom drives again. Although we reached the races on the occasion of which I write, the effort was in vain as the horse I was hoping to run had forgotten her passport and was turned back at the starting gate. But at Doncaster, leading from start to finish, she won an auction plate by some six lengths and four hundred pounds for me.

Money counts, I am not the man to pretend it doesn't. But it is difficult to describe the ecstasy of seeing one's horse win a race. It is a pleasure to be savoured not only because of its rarity but because one has done nothing whatever to deserve the prize.

One hasn't bred it or broken it, trained it or ridden it, and only bought it because no one else would. Suddenly you stand beside it in the winners' enclosure avoiding its hooves and basking in its reflected glory. Your horse has run before, probably more than once, and all sorts of excuses have been put forward and accepted as to why it finished where it did. She hadn't liked the starter's assistant, she had been put off by a bumpy journey, possibly a bumpy race. She isn't the sort that likes going round bends or being too far in front, which she never was, or too far behind, which is why she nearly stopped altogether. You drive home from the track questioning the prudence in keeping such a sad ugly duckling and then, suddenly, on a summer evening in Doncaster, with the crowd roaring and champagne corks beginning to pop, she turns into a swan.

There are two sorts of rewards in life: those that come through effort and concentration and dedication and hard work, and those that come out of the blue heaven, which surprise you at the actual prize-giving but which later, on sober reflection, you expected all the time. Providence is on my side, you tell yourself. I never doubted it, and stride on once more, a giant refreshed by sheer luck.

The second time I remember Providence actually taking a hand where I was concerned, was at school. When sitting one day in my usual black despair and almost unable to swallow the Wednesday mince, my housemaster summoned me to his side and announced he was sending me home for the rest of the term. I went home for the rest of my life. But why? Why did the lightning strike that particular afternoon? Why, an hour later, was I standing on the platform of Wellington College station, my playbox secured, my ticket in my pocket, gazing fearfully along the track lest I woke up before the engine arrived?

I have never discovered. But I have never forgotten one moment of the day's happenings, or ceased to believe, like Logan Pearsall Smith, that I am on occasions, and for strictly limited periods, God's Ewe Lamb.

I was a good deal older on the third occasion. I was a small-part actor with a good deal of spare time on my hands and I had, like most actors, written a play. And although it had been turned down by everyone who read it, it was suddenly accepted by a great West End star who I can only think hadn't read it at all because she subsequently insisted on my re-writing practically every line. But accept it she did, and asked me to luncheon and gave me a cheque for a hundred pounds with the coffee. And I walked out of her house on air and collided heavily with a pillar box. Once again, I expected to wake up and found I had already done so and was still clutching the cheque. The house disappeared in the war, along with my benefactor, but the pillar box is still there, a private shrine which I never fail to touch in reverence and gratitude each time I pass it.

Once Providence had got me married and arranged the family, I don't pretend that I was on my own exactly, but his sudden appearances became rather a thing of the past. True, there was the curious case of Joan Tetzel, whom I used to work with in radio in New York before the war. One day, twenty years later, I read the script of a play called *The Little*

Hut and told the producer that if he could find her again I would do the play.

'But she's gone,' I warned him. 'Vanished into American thin air.'

'Not at all, she was in my office this morning, wondering what on earth had happened to you,' he told me.

Then, twenty years later again, almost to the day, the same thing happened. I conjured up her name at luncheon with my agent and met her an hour later in a picture gallery. Neither of us had heard or thought of each other in the meantime.

That sort of thing doesn't require much effort on the part of Providence, I imagine, but I am always setting him greater challenges. Every so often I receive mysterious letters from unknown Irish publicans inviting me to buy sweepstake tickets, and I fill out the coupons, copy the address, add the five pounds, stick down the envelope and hold it up for Providence in case he's watching. He never seems to be. Then, too, I sometimes tempt Providence to meet me in a fun spot – Las Vegas, Monte Carlo, or nearer home. You'll find me, I tell him, at the second table on the right, just at the back of the 'Dorch'. I suppose, like me, he leads a busy life.

But if I ever think myself neglected, I do well to remember the first time we met on a summer afternoon in Folkestone, Kent. As usual in those days, I didn't know what on earth to do with myself, only that I didn't want to play cricket, and I somehow managed to slip away unnoticed from the dreaded sound of bat and ball and my hated companions. I walked in no particular direction (or so I thought), past the bandstand and the lifts which moved surprisingly down the cliff face to the pier and the roller skating rink beneath, and I turned my back on the sea and my face towards the shops, planning to buy myself a half pound of chocolate biscuits of which I was, even in those days, extravagantly fond. But when I reached the grocery shop it was closed. Next door to it stood the Pleasure Gardens Theatre and a poster advertising Charles Macdonald's production of Shaw's *The Doctor's Dilemma*, with Esmé Percy, and across it a sticker announcing EXTRA MATINEE-TODAY. Providence reached in my pocket for the shilling I had saved for the biscuits and in a moment I was at the back of the gallery.

The Theatre had the strangest smell and, although I had never experienced it before and this was my first visit to a play, I recognised the scent of pleasure. There was a string orchestra already playing in the pit and the bottom of the curtain was lit by the footlights. I wondered what on earth lay on the other side. How was I to know, until it rose, that it was home?

REFLECTIONS
IN
A
DRESSING-ROOM
MIRROR

The Bluffer

'Never go on the stage laddie, without first saying to yourself – Ladies and Gentlemen, if you think you can do this better yourself, come up and try.' It was the first piece of helpful advice on acting I ever received. I'm not sure it wasn't the only one.

Bluff or confidence? Artists need both and only a narrow line divides them. I remember Balmain designing a dress for Joan Tetzel, in a play called *The Little Hut*. The dress looked as if it had come out of a bandbox instead of the sea. Nobody dared to touch it and then the master arrived. Taking a penknife, he casually slashed it into rags. Beautiful rags, mind you, the sort of rags Cinderella changes out of to go to the ball. Could anyone but Balmain have done it? Certainly no one but Balmain would have dared.

What we all crave, in life, in art, on television, in government, is the expert. Some experts are, by the nature of their calling, self-appointed. All surgeons are experts, most dentists, some criminal lawyers. The bigger the expert, the greater the bluff. The more we have to pay them, the more confidence they inspire in us. The bluff of price is the most effective bluff of all.

The first time I went to Hollywood was to play the part of the dauphin in *Marie Antoinette*. Up to then my film career had been a disaster. I had been hired twice previously and sacked on both occasions after the first day for gross incompetence. My agent knew this. MGM knew it, too. When my agent told MGM my price, they roared with laughter. 'How come?' they asked him. 'He's never earned a sausage. He's never lasted 24 hours. So how is it he's worth $500 a week?'

'He's not,' agreed my agent. 'But he doesn't want to go to America and he has a large personal fortune.' The bluff lasted until I'd signed the contract, but then I had to ask for some cash to get to the boat. Each contract has been a game of poker since then.

It is more important for an actor to learn to bluff than to learn to act. All the great figures on the world stage have one thing in common: an ability to make the public rub its eyes. Now you see it, now you don't.

How good a pianist is Liberace? If you didn't know it was Andy Williams singing, would you listen? Or Gregory Peck acting, would you watch? You might and then again you might not.

Certainly, the greater the star the less he need do to preserve his own image. The public will shine and polish it for him every day. They will tell you that a great artist learns to throw away the rule book. 'Watch the sheer economy of the man,' the public tells itself. 'He does nothing.'

But a word of caution, gentle watcher. Never, never be tempted to bluff about not wanting the job. The bluff of resignation is one which by its very nature will almost certainly be called. No matter how valuable an employee or how faithful a friend you may be, no matter how great your knowledge of where the body is buried, if you offer to resign you can bet your bottom dollar your resignation will be accepted. You are presenting your partner or your employer with a temptation he cannot resist.

I remember my stupefaction when I once told a manager who was employing me at the time that if the director stayed I must leave. 'You're both going,' he chortled. I learnt my lesson. I have never again offered my resignation on any terms. If they want to fire me, by God, they'll have to pay.

Miss Missouri and Miss Parker

I am descended from a long line of furniture arrangers. I lived much of my youth in furnished houses and long before the family had unpacked, my father would be in the parlour of our new quarters, impatient to begin shifting the piano. 'Just catch hold of your end, Dai,' he would urge my mother, who was called Daisy in real life – as much of it as she enjoyed with Father, at any rate. 'Just catch hold of your end and we'll try it over here.' Hours later, after every stick of furniture had been re-arranged at least three times and the dining-room table brought in from the dining-room to see if that would help, my father would consent to the rest of the family putting everything back as it was when he walked in, and depart in search of the nearest bridge club.

Similarly, when faced with the need to do yet another play I find what I most enjoy is re-siting the make-up table in my dressing-room. 'Over here,' I urge the property master, interrupted from more immediate chores. 'Over here, there's a good chap and we'll have the cheval mirror so, and the armchair in the corner.' The arrangement completed, I find the door no longer opens and the dressing-table mirror in darkness owing to a scarcity of electric points. Eventually we are back where we started, and to the altogether more mundane matter of discovering whether I know my lines, but how I've enjoyed it all . . .

'We have a rowing eight,' the director assured me, 'and we are jacking up your seat. That way the camera can see the water and the Houses of Parliament. Just come into shot as if you were taking a stroll, sit down and let us have it in twenty-eight seconds.' Behind me on the Embankment were assembled other actors, dressed as policemen, American tourists and babies. The period is early Coward, late Cochran. There is a good deal of discussion about the light, and whether Big Ben looks prettier through the mist, or would it be wise to wait for the sun to shine, supposing it ever

181

does? Finally we go ahead, the rowing crew is positioned, the cameras turn over, and there am I, as large as life and striving to be as natural, inviting all and sundry to a one-week London Show Tour next winter, the price of the air fare to include the hotel, theatre tickets, a car for a day and a Polaroid camera. 'If I didn't live here,' I conclude, 'I'd take it myself.'

Towards evening they seemed satisfied, and I bade everyone goodbye and walked over the bridge and through the park past the grebes on the lake, and waited outside Swan and Edgars until there was a break in the traffic. It was here that I met her, a school-teacher from Missouri on the sort of package deal I had just been advertising, and actually coming to my theatre that evening. Could I, she asked me, tell her where the theatre was? I thought it prudent to conduct her in person. Who knew what other actors might be lurking around, plying for casual trade?

It was the hour when the young take over the Circus, spilling out onto the roadway, squatting on doorsteps, draining their Coca Cola tins to the last drop, camouflaging themselves like stick insects amid the prevailing squalor. What can one say to an American school-teacher about the city we have pulled down about our ears, how apologise for the filth, the litter, the stench of the hot dog stands? Years ago it was the British abroad who held their handkerchiefs to their noses and marvelled at the state of the natives, but now it is Miss Missouri's turn to walk delicately.

I took her almost to the doors of the Lyric, but not quite, for I knew there was half an hour for her to wait before they opened. How would she pass the time, I wondered. Spend it, perhaps, exploring the little alleyways at the back of the theatre, or examining the photographs outside rival establishments. She might even prepare for herself a map of this part of theatreland against the time she would perhaps venture into it again.

In the press, theatres are listed alphabetically and their locations withheld, presumably because this is the least helpful arrangement possible. If there is a boom in theatreland, it is certainly not due to any effort on the part of the bricks and mortar men. The ground landlords remain blissfully unaware of any responsibility they might owe the public. When she does gain access to the building, Miss Missouri will notice it is far from being air conditioned. She will be fortunate, should she decide to buy herself a drink, to find ice available; she will certainly not be offered iced water. No one here has heard of the sort of dispenser so common in the States, or if they have, they have recoiled in horror at the expense of installing one. There's no money in that, they have told themselves. Give them cold water and they won't touch the tepid orangeade at ten pence a cardboard carton we peddle in the interval. It's the same with the programme. If you want to know what the play is about, who's in it and where it takes place, they're not going to tell you for nothing. All you get is what you've paid for – a seat – and sometimes, on busy evenings if there's been a double booking, not even that.

I wondered where Miss Missouri had bought her ticket. At a library, no doubt. She would have had to pay a bit more for it, but it's simpler than trying to find the theatre twice in one day. There was just a chance, I supposed, that Miss Missouri had contacted Miss Parker herself.

In the days when London theatres were patronised by the indigent rich, Miss Parker held supreme sway at the most lordly of all the agencies. To her Bond Street premises flocked the fashionable and lively, in order that she might plot their social activities from Christmas to Goodwood. She snapped up the best seats at the Circus, the Horseshow, the Royal Tournament, arranged Centre Court seats for Wimbledon, boxes for Ascot, coaches for Eton and Harrow, launches for Henley, and was always cajoling, bullying, beseeching her customers to spend their evenings at the theatre. 'Of course you won't be tired, dear,' she would tell them. 'I've got a box for you at the Strand. If you don't stay for the last race, you'll be back in time for the Palace, I've managed to get you six returns. You'll want to go to the first night at the Savoy, they say it's most amusing, leave it to me.' If I or any other actor approached her during working hours, she would draw us into the act. 'Here,' she would tell startled patrons, 'is Mr. Morley himself, now you'll want to see *his* play, of course, *very* clever. I know you're only up for three days, but what are you doing Thursday? Oh, of course, I've got you tickets for the Opera. Well, you'll want to do something in the afternoon. You have a matinée, Mr. Morley, haven't you? Splendid. Hang on and I'll get on to the Box Office.' As often as not, it worked.

Her enthusiasm and expertise was boundless. I think only once did she ever speak sharply to me, and that was when I essayed a serious play about religion. 'Leave that sort of thing to Sir Alec,' she begged, 'your public doesn't expect you to handle it. I'm not even trying to sell tickets, they'd be shocked.' But times have changed for Miss Parker as they have for all of us. Her one-time clients seldom go to a theatre in London nowadays; they are too old or too deaf, they can't afford it or can't be bothered. It's difficult to get to London, it's difficult to park the motor, it's difficult to hear, and above all, there's the telly. So Miss Parker, like the rest of us, relies on Miss Missouri, and very grateful we are to her and to her courage and boundless enthusiasm which propels her along the streets at dusk, asking, and seldom being told, the exact whereabouts of the

Fortune or the Comedy or even Drury Lane. It's not that they don't want to tell her, it's just that most of the Greeks or Arabs of whom she enquires are strangers here themselves. It's no good asking the British, they too are only down for the day. As for the policemen, they are so besotted with their portable radios that they will only seize the opportunity to call back to London Central and chat up the Desk Sergeant, who ten to one won't be able to hear them properly. If Miss Missouri wants to know where anything is in London, she should always ask a Chinaman. It's a very old civilisation; besides, there are as yet no Chinese tourists.

Where Angels Fear to Tread

A bachelor friend of mine who persistently invests in theatrical productions attended a cocktail party the other evening, where his hostess persisted in introducing him to all and sundry as a 'professional fairy'. 'Luckily,' he told me when recounting the incident, 'that sort of thing causes very little embarrassment nowadays.' I don't know whether in his role of angel my friend makes money, but at least it gives him an interest when he goes to plays for which he has provided some of the bread. He doesn't have to follow the plot. He can be counting the house. Like the prudent angel he is, he makes a point of spreading his wings. It is nearly always fatal to put all your eggs in one basket.

About theatrical brokers I must write carefully. Most of them have employed me at one time or another, and I am always mindful they may have to do so again. Yet honesty compels me to point out that very few of them really know their business. That is not to say they won't make money for their angels on odd occasions, but it will always be the odd occasions. You won't have much chance of getting in on the ground floor unless the management concerned already suspects there is a flood in the basement. You are unlikely, therefore, to be asked to invest in a Palladium pantomime or the 'Black and White Minstrel Show'. Such rich pastures are strictly reserved. But supposing you have a few pounds to invest and would like a flutter. How should you proceed? I am assuming that you haven't a mistress whose talent you propose to diversify. In easier days there was always a place in the chorus for a pretty miss, provided her financial backing was in order, but times and choruses have changed. Another friend of mine whose belle amie is currently appearing in *Oh Calcutta* is always boasting of how pretty she looks with her clothes on.

Let us return to our moutons, and apologise for the French which keeps creeping in. Angels, I fear, are constantly associated in my mind with the belle époque. Let us consider where your money – if not safe, that would be asking too much – at least has a sporting chance of survival, and even multiplying. Should you go for the big spender who at the first hint of your interest, the first sight of your cheque book, wines and dines you at Burke's or Scotts or the Grand Véfour? 'Steady with the Château Lafitte,' you tell yourself, 'this chap will spend the ready in pre-production expenses. He will be back to demand the company's rail fare to Southsea.' At least you will have a better time in his company than you will with one of the more austere brethren who lives in a poky little attic on top of his theatre, with minimal furniture and mature lady typists. 'No room here,' you tell yourself, 'for the casting couch', and you are right. If caution reassures you, go for one of these. To my mind you might as well have your money in a building society for all the fun you are likely to get out of it. You will, of course, be sent tickets for the first night, but you will also be expected to pay for them.

No, what you need when you are starting out on your journey along the celestial way, is a little man who has the time — because until he's got your cheque in his bank account business isn't all that brisk — to show you round the stables, and introduce you to some of the colts and possibly fillies. He may even encourage you to read some scripts and get your advice on the casting, enquiring whether you would prefer Larry or Paul, and when you express surprise that either of these gentlemen is available, you will be further surprised to learn that he gave both of them their first job, and that they would do anything for him, if asked.

Eventually, if you have taken my advice and your cheque has been cleared, you may find yourself invited to a pre-production party to meet the actors who are about to rehearse your play. You will find that not only are Olivier and Scofield missing, but that you have never heard of a single member of the cast. The mood on these occasions is one of hysterical over-confidence. In the abandoned ballroom in which the first rehearsal is to take place, you are uncertain where to put down your emptied champagne glass, and are probably still clutching it as you tiptoe away, unwilling to interrupt the proceedings any longer. If this lot can get away with it, you tell yourself, it will be a miracle. But in the role of angel you should expect miracles. They are not likely to happen, of course, but you should expect them.

Depending on the size of your investment and the amount of spare time and cash you still have available, you may attend the world première of the piece when it opens in Cheltenham, and be amazed how little excitement is generated on this auspicious occasion. You will have to be constantly telling yourself that from little acorns mighty oak trees grow, if you wish to keep up your courage. Monday night is never very brisk in the provinces, and nothing alerts your would-be theatregoer in the tall grass and persuades him to leave his car in the garage and himself in the parlour more than that fatal announcement on the bills: 'Prior to immediate London production'. Granted that Cheltenham is not exactly the right venue for the piece, and it is unlikely to be properly understood by the natives, everyone agrees afterwards at a party held in the local bistro, that there were one or two good early laughs and the play held up even if the audience didn't. It needs cutting, the management insist. Cutting is the panacea invariably prescribed after a first night, even if it isn't always applied to the patient. Managements insist on cutting, just as at one time physicians insisted on bleeding. Most plays are sickly at birth, and many succumb at a surprisingly early age. Euthanasia is by no means uncommon, but no such fate awaits your little piece apparently. After Cheltenham, a week at Bognor is planned and then there is talk of Richmond, immediately prior to its arrival in the West End.

After Richmond, however, everyone suddenly decides to go to Southsea. It seems that the London theatre cannot yet be announced to the impatient West End patrons, as the play currently playing there still refuses to complete two consecutive weeks below its stop figure. But everyone confidently expects it to fold once the Motor Show is over. Southsea comes and goes, and then rather surprisingly Billingham, and by now you are in overcall, that is to say the original subscribed capital having been exhausted by unexpectedly heavy losses on the road, everyone is expected to divvy up again. You are absolutely sick of the play, and just when you are hoping you have heard the last of it, the phone rings and your manager is on the blower to tell you he has a West End theatre and all signals are 'Go, go', but there is the question of a further overcall, and will you be sure to let him know how many seats you want for the First Night, and the rush is on. He also apologises in advance for the fact that some of your party may have to be accommodated in the Circle. You tell him that your party will consist simply of your wife and yourself, and what with all the money you have spent already you couldn't possibly afford more than two seats in the Upper Circle. But on this occasion the seats are free, it seems, and when yours arrive you will find you have been accommodated with eight pairs of stalls. You have considerable difficulty getting rid of them.

On the whole, perhaps it would be better if you stayed at home that night yourself. If you do decide to attend, you will be in for a shock. First nights are not what they were. The prevailing mood can be likened to that of a first-class railway carriage whose passengers are not expecting the ticket collector to come along. Except for the critics, a faceless coterie of railway employees travelling first because it is one of the perks, no one appears to be exactly at ease. Here and there the season ticket holders add a little reassurance and there is a sprinkling of the more flamboyant characters in showbiz, some of them in evening dress – or what passes for evening dress nowadays if you have time to puzzle it out. There must surely be a man who designs clothes for such occasions, a sort of Teddy Tinling of the centre foyer.

The play is received ecstatically. You leave the theatre telling yourself that you are in the money, and the next morning the critics tear it to shreds while the management is busy tearing their notices to shreds to extract a few quotes to paste up outside the theatre. When the play comes off in a month, the final balance sheet shows a deficit of £78, but it seems you are not to be asked to fork out any further sum, and you breathe a sigh of relief and send the letter on to your accountant. You might have done worse. After all, it takes a long time to learn to play the harp.

Happy as a Badger

Whenever there is an audience to watch him, the donkey in the Well House of Carisbrooke Castle leaves his dressing-room and, mounting the tread wheel, accomplishes a journey of three hundred yards in it while contriving to remain in exactly the same place. A bucket of water is thus raised approximately 161 feet from the bottom of the well and the contents inspected, after which the water is returned to the well and the donkey, acknowledging the polite applause, returns to his dressing-room until his next performance.

Perspicacious readers will have drawn the parallel but, I trust, not anticipated the question I am anxious to pose. Does the donkey enjoy himself, and if so, why? He certainly enjoys the biscuits which his visitors feed him, warm quarters and the company of other donkeys in the cast with whom he shares the work, and we are assured that the work suits the animals and one is recorded to have died at the ripe age (for a donkey) of forty-nine years. I am now sixty-six and I've enjoyed it; but it is an odd occupation though not unique, of course: there are other actors in theatres all over the world just as there are other treadmills motivated by donkeys. You can train a donkey apparently in three months: how long does it take to train an actor? Or are they better self-taught? From now on we shall be discussing only the theatre, so donkey lovers had better get off here.

Unlike most of my distinguished colleagues, and having been in the profession a bare forty-six years, I have reached no hard and fast conclusion on this or any other aspect of the trade. But I cannot help remarking that the more seriously an actor takes himself and his work, the more dedicated he appears; the more determined he is as he grows older to enlarge his scope, to accept new challenges, to break new ground, the less time he spends actually doing so. With the possible exception of Gielgud, who is ever ready to have a go, and Burton, who is ever going to be ready to do so, actors like Scofield, Guinness, Finney, Redgrave, Williamson, Stephens — all of whom are on record as finding a dedication in their vocation which has eluded me – appear at infrequent intervals and usually for limited runs. They actually enjoy learning new parts and rehearsing them – some of them even enjoy being directed by such insatiable sado-masochists as Peter Brook, who is so entirely wrapped up in the mystique of the impossible dream that he now has his actor victims running around market places in Teheran, talking gibberish to the bewildered stall holders and bored chauffeurs polishing their masters' motors in the sun and trying to listen to local football scores on their radios.

When I first left school, which I hated, and went onto the stage, which I loved, I was visited almost immediately by an ex-chum, indeed the sole chum I ever made at Wellington College. He seemed puzzled by my choice of career, and searching for a clue as to why I was immured in such uncomfortable surroundings as the meanest dressing-room of the County Theatre, Reading, opined that once the curtain had fallen we were obviously up each other like knives. It wasn't quite true, even in those days, but I think I prefer the public to think of us as belonging to what a British judge referred to this week as 'the knickers and gin crowd' than to the culture-vulture crowd. Our life can hardly be described as a very sober one. Would you like your daughter to marry an actor? Of course not. We have a higher divorce rate than in most professions – just below dentists in the league table, actually. We spend a good deal of our life out of work, sitting around waiting for our agent to call, and when he does find us a job, it is not even intended to last long. Television is a matter usually of three weeks' filming, often just days. We are always begging the public to watch when often there is really little to see. The theatre was more successful, certainly, when we resolutely declined to take Hamlet's advice to hold a mirror up to nature. Hamlet was a perfect fool. Every clown wants to play Hamlet, I wanted to myself once but I would have played him for what he is – a clown. It's too late now, thank goodness, and I have few ambitions left. One which is common to most of us, I suppose, is the wish that once, in an empty theatre, whilst we are rehearsing a new play on an empty stage, the cleaning lady at the back of the stalls will stop thumping the seats and emptying the ashtrays and generally banging around as cleaning ladies do, and, her task abandoned, sit helpless and spellbound, just watching and listening. It's only the cleaning woman I wish to hold in my spell, not the ordinary men and women who come willingly in the evenings and pay for admission. I don't mind what they do, they can kiss and cuddle and rustle chocolates and sleep peacefully, they can come as late as they please and leave as early. I have their money, I am there if they need me, but I shall be no whit affronted if they don't. I like, of course, to keep

190

some sort of control: I prefer the majority at least to stay awake and watchful, I want to make you laugh. I am, after all, very fond of you, and why shouldn't I be? You've been very good to me for close on fifty years. When I let you down, you were forgiving, and when I didn't, you seemed grateful and even congratulated me. Tradesmen are not often congratulated: a man may spend a lifetime serving the public and count on one hand the customers who have praised his butter.

Yet people come up to me on railway platforms and tell me they have enjoyed the play. True, they add that 'these days they can do with a laugh', they've been saying that, too, for fifty years. 'Why?' I sometimes enquire, 'What's so terrible about today?' They never tell me, and all those years I don't really believe I've ever really wanted to know.

It's because we actors are tradesmen and not artists that our life on the whole is such a happy one. Artists have it rough: you can paint all your life and never sell a picture; you can write music and never hear it played, or a book and never hold it in your hand; but an actor gets instant recognition though, alas, no longer instant oblivion. Before pictures, who doubted Irving? But now, with his films still orbiting in space, who believes Charlton Heston? Yet Mr. Heston is the very man who appeals for funds to buy up old pictures, other people's as well as his own, let's be fair, and preserve them. Perish the thought, and ever better, perish the actor. Our performances live on in the memory of the faithful; they are safer than in a bank vault. On the staircase of my club there is a chair on which Irving is supposed to have died. He had been touring around the provinces. He was old and tired and sick. He gave his last performance to a rather meagre audience, somehow managed to get back to the hotel where he was staying, sat down in the hall and died. Should actors go on until they drop? I think so. Climbing the stairs on my way to the bar, I look at the chair and I remember what Irving once said to Ellen Terry when she asked him what he had got out of a life of endless theatrical activity. 'A few friends, dear, and a whisky and soda whenever I wanted one; what else is there to get?' Irving had no folie de grandeur about his trade. True, when after a successful first night his wife, who didn't care much for the business, asked him how much longer he proposed to go on with this nonsense, Henry stopped the hansom they were sharing and got out for ever. Well, I suppose he may have ridden in the cab again; by that time he probably wanted to leave his wife anyway. Actors' wives say worse things to them than that. Sometimes we leave them, sometimes we don't. Meeting Rex Harrison once in the Burlington Arcade – where you'd expect him to be – he was kind enough to congratulate me on a television programme I had done the night before. It was an instalment of the ever popular feature 'This Is Your Life'. For an egomaniac like myself it is well nigh the perfect programme – as long as I am the one whose life they are discussing. Rex seemed to think that on this occasion I had got away with it. 'And why not?' he continued. 'You've been so sensible; one house, one wife and, if you'll forgive me saying so, one performance.'

Actually, he is wrong about the house, but we have lived in it for thirty-five years now. It is just the right distance from London – about thirty miles – and I drive up each evening as the commuters are returning to the Thames Valley along the motorway. Their side of the road is choked with traffic, mine comparatively clear. When I come home, both sides are trouble-free, and between the motorway and my house are country lanes I share with foxes and deer and the occasional badger.

A few friends, a whisky and soda, and an opportunity to greet a badger. 'Why are you fond of badgers?' you will ask, if you've read this far, and to be honest I am not particularly fond of badgers and I would be scared stiff if I met one on foot, but it makes a good curtain to the day. We lead a funny sort of life, we nocturnals, but my goodness don't we enjoy it.

That's why, when I'm asked, I tell people I'm feeling just fine – happy as a badger.